White River
Junctions

White River Junctions

2nd Edition

This edition contains approximately 50 fewer pages than the first edition. This is by virtue of reformatting. No text has been cut, though some facts have been added or updated. The photographs are also new.

This is a work of nonfiction. All resemblance of facts, locations, and subjects to fictionalized creations is strictly accidental.

We founded f/**64** Publishing to promote crisp, clear storytelling that captures those details essential to understanding a subject. Like making a photographic exposure at f/64, this takes time and strategy…and can result in breathtaking work. The company is named in honor of the association of photographers co-founded by Ansel Adams: Group f.64.

f/**64** Publishing
197 Pine St. Suite 34 | Portland, ME 04102 USA
www.f64publishing.com
www.whiteriverjunctions.com

1. History-Regional-New England
2. Biography
3. Dave Norman-Essays

ISBN 13:978-0-9831858-0-2
Written and published in the USA

*For Joe Pogar, Dot Jones, Harold Wright,
Larry Chase, and Winona Hary*

Also by Dave Norman

501 Paintball Tips, Tricks, and Tactics

A Small Town Celebration

Following Josh

Leading Jake

www.davenorman.net

www.f64publishing.com

Contents

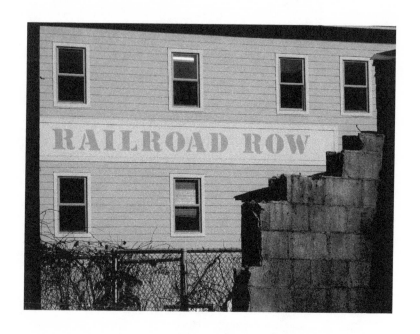

Railroad Row—A modern building on the old "Railroad Row," as seen through the ruined wall of an older building.

Foreword

I was hungry and the local restaurants knew me a little too well, so I drove west across the Connecticut River to a town I'd never visited before: White River Junction, Vermont, where my epicurean adventure went awry.

That's because in 2004 there were only two restaurants in the little village that were open of an evening. Being a stranger, I couldn't find either of them. What I found, alone on autumn-darkened streets, was much more important.

* * * * *

South Main Street is a one-way affair that curves around the Gates Block, past the entrance to the Hotel Coolidge, past the former Post Office, and out of town through what used to be called the "Italian Section." Most of the lights were out; the town was dark and cold. I walked down the middle of the street without disrupting any traffic whatsoever.

The storefronts looked hollow and vacant, and the buildings—beautiful brick buildings, one made of granite blocks with wrought iron, all heavy with the weight of history—had the look of museum pieces. They looked important, but I didn't feel that I could touch them...or gain anything by trying, each one's history theirs alone and as remote as artifacts in glass cases.

Where had all the people gone? Why were the buildings, so large and important-looking, so quiet and dark? Was the town abandoned, or waiting to be filled?

As I walked the wrong way up the middle of South Main Street, hoping in vain to find a burger joint, I remembered a painful conversation with a college freshman earlier that day. I was a graduate student at the time, barely older than him, yet we had little in common. Our references seemed a generation apart. Then I made the mistake of trying to give him advice.

He didn't hear a word I said; he just stared blankly ahead as if I was speaking Chinese to the clouds. It was a look I recognized—the same one I wore on family trips to see old relatives. I couldn't relate to their lives, any more than I could relate to the plain facts and dull writing in history textbooks. It was all "pre me." Pre Teenage Mutant Ninja Turtles®, which is year zero so far as my life is concerned.

Reality, you see, did not exist before I was born.

Maybe you can relate.

But then there are dinosaur bones, and my grandfather's scars, and my dad's pocketknife from when he was a boy, all these things which suggest that maybe life did exist before me.

That conversation with the freshman, though... Couldn't he see that I had already been where he was, and might have learned a thing or two about it?

Still, he shut me out, just as I shut out most of the world before my time. But there, on the street in White River Junction, it felt as if history for once was the one alienating me from its conversation. The vacant façades looked like backs turned towards me.

Which was the point when I realized that I could

see my life as mere history to others, doomed to be abstracted into a cold remoteness until the "me" is gone from it forever, or I could see history as a collection of lives like mine—the beautiful and meaningful lives of other people, and even places and ideas. Then the town around me filled with voices thankful to be heard.

I understood that buildings have histories, just like I do; that ideas have life cycles and succeed or fail just like people. Perhaps in the stories of lives already lived, generations come and gone, I might find some guidance for those big questions I ask.

Perish the thought, I might learn something!

But the epiphany I had in the middle of that darkened street was about more than seeing the essential value of history…it was about feeling personally connected to it, if I just recognize the humanity of those who have gone before me and listen, really listen, to the whispers in the air.

At the least, history might explain why I couldn't find a burger in what seemed like a once-thriving town.

So I took a new look around White River Junction and saw the same stoic buildings and dark, lifeless windows in brand new terms: as books to read by the light of morning. As keepers of stories, life stories like mine—histories made real. It was a true revelation.

* * * * *

This book began as work for my Master's Degree at Dartmouth College, just a few miles by canoe north of White River Junction. The more I learned about the town, the more I came to see its story as a beautiful illustration of American history—an abstract concept, to be sure, but one that made increasing sense as I linked local events to national ones. Touring the buildings, meeting old railroad men, feeling the cracks in the brick, made the past come alive for me…and then it started to truly make sense.

In the 1800s the railroad turned wild western outposts into boomtowns…as it did to White River Junction here in Vermont. The culture of celebration, war-wealth, and hope that came out of World War I set the country up for the Great Depression…whose effects I had read about in broad terms, but heard about firsthand from several of the men I interviewed. The suffragettes of the Women's Liberation Movement made national headlines, while local gym teacher Dorothy Mock worked to get girl's high school athletic teams equal opportunities as those for the boys. Joe Pogar played fiddle in speakeasies during Prohibition.

I had read about all this before, idly turning the pages without much sinking in…it was all too abstract. But here, in White River Junction—this tiny village not many people outside New England have ever heard of—I saw how the railroad transformed the streets I walked and the buildings I toured, heard firsthand stories of great fires, found the kind of touchstones that make history first accessible, and then meaningful.

Which is why I turned that initial research into this book—to present a little Vermont town on a humble stage where you can watch some of the biggest ideas from the last century and a half play out…and actually get something out of it. I did.

So welcome to White River Junction, the way I found it during my research (from 2005 to 2007), and the way it came to be…

the
Buildings

Top: White River Station as it appears today

Bottom: An excursion train that rode the tracks north towards Norwich for the "Glory Days Festival."

Glory Days of the Railroad

Dawn breaks this morning over White River Junction, Vermont, with mountain fog rolling through the town along the railroad right-of-way. I walk between two glistening steel rails, silver-topped from dew and polished from a century and a half in service. The ties beneath my feet are a short pace apart, the heavy, creosote-soaked wood pushed flush with the gravel. My *plomp, plomp* along the tracks sets a rhythm like the clack, clack of wheels as I walk south through the north yard, nearing the fifth incarnation of their Union Station—past the faded memories on worn buildings; towards the glory days of the railroad.

Buttery mountain sunshine makes the trees and buildings glow—the former to my left, the latter to my right as I walk between the rails. I pass the Tip Top Building with the pockmarked and faded Tip Top Bakery advertisement painted on red bricks. The girl in the ad peeks into a plastic bag of "Tip Top Enriched White Bread," her words—"It's like opening the ___ to a bakery"—interrupted by a window cut into the wall. The Tip Top Bakery closed decades ago. Walking deeper south, the logo of the Ward Baking Company—painted farther down the long Tip Top Building—advertises a business that folded even earlier. I am on my way to the railroad station to meet Chris McKinley, the building's self-described "volunteer agent and honorary historian."

A hundred years ago I could not have walked here for all the trains barreling through from somewhere; today the rails are quiet, trains passing hours apart and leaving me safe to wander their tracks past long-quiet loading docks. A few days ago I interviewed Mike Farnsworth and Howard Logan, two gentlemen who worked for the Boston and Maine line. Howard gave me a good history of the railroad, Mike filled in the details, and they pointed out a few good books. I've met with the curator of the Main Street Museum in the old firehouse on Bridge Street, David Fairbanks Ford, who explained how that old bakery in the Tip Top Building was so intrinsically tied to the rail yard…and the fate of White River Junction. Their voices murmur in the back of my mind, just under the *plomp, plomp* as I continue onwards to meet with Chris.

White River Junction's story is that of the railroad, two wars, the Great Depression, and other things I need to learn—and care—more about before I can really understand the town…before I can really understand how communities are made, lost, and rebuilt. The history of the railroad here is the same as in so many small mountain villages, from Vermont to Colorado, plains communities like my hometown in Illinois, and the places in between; learning about one place helps me understand many more. Mike pointed that out.

This steel road leads me past an antique furniture store, between piles of spikes and tracks and fasteners rusting and crumbling into the gravel, beyond the charred basement hole of a building recently burned, under a modern sign that says "Railroad Row," onwards south—south towards the station and back through time more than one hundred fifty years.

* * * * *

This was once a wide spot on an Indian trail that settlers came to call Lyman's Point. It was a place where you could put in a canoe or raft and cross to the east, or to the northern section of the Province of New York—later called the Republic of Vermont, and now called, simply, Vermont. Lyman's Point was at the confluence of what also came to be known as the Connecticut and White Rivers, along which lumberjacks and river men flowed logs from lumber camps up north on their ways ever south to paper and lumber mills. The settlement grew very slowly, aided by footbridges that spanned the White River, and gained the name White River Village.

The truly intrepid could canoe—as John Ledyard famously did in or around 1773—from that region south as far as Long Island Sound, and by such means access the ocean if they didn't mind a number of portages. Sources indicate there was a certain amount of river traffic, of the canoe type with some flat-bottom barges, that plied stretches of the Connecticut River, and larger craft farther south. When it froze in the winter, horses could be ridden up and down the ice.

But then the rails transformed America, and connected the village all the way west to California and south to the Gulf of Mexico. Fast, reliable freight and passenger service shrank the distance between towns, making the village a neighbor to cities throughout the United States. People and material came in from everywhere, goods could be sent out anywhere, and a new era dawned.

But first, the railroad had to get there...

* * * * *

In 1830 there were twenty-three miles of railroad track in the entire country, according to former Dartmouth College president E.M. Hopkins in a 1938 speech. Along their twin rails chugged massive steam-powered, wood-fed locomotives that each pulled fewer than ten forty-foot, wood-side boxcars. Then miles of track were added and steam powered trains improved, establishing a bold new concept in shipping and transportation that sparked wild speculation across the country. When workers drove the final iron spike into the Albany-Schenectady Railroad through New York in 1831, rumors blossomed about a railway connecting the port cities with Montreal via Vermont. Speculators convened in Windsor, Vermont, in 1836 to discuss a rail line through the Connecticut River Valley.

A survey team charted a course north through what was then called White River Village, a tiny cluster of buildings south of Hartford and just below the confluence of the White and Connecticut rivers. The crew reported their survey in Boston on November 10th, 1844: such a line was possible.

The railroad would mean new jobs for Vermonters, new income for the state, and new opportunities for businesses isolated by the rigors of overland mountain travel. Also, the railroad could bring more heating fuel (coal) to the region, and take lumber away to mills in markets far from the Connecticut River log drives. For Boston, a rail line through Vermont meant access to Green Mountain timber, Canadian markets, and rural markets—for agricultural goods, paper and lumber form the inland mills, wool and other goods—in an ever-expanding network through New England. With the assistance of well-heeled speculators, Vermont legislators and business-men drafted a charter to create the Connecticut River Railroad Company; it was signed in the Vermont capital on November 5th, 1845.

Two businesses built the railroad through Vermont: the Connecticut and Passumpsic Rivers Railroad Company operated the northern section, towards Canada and Lake Champlain, and the Connecticut River Railroad Company operated the southern section, connecting with other New England railways. The division between them was roughly halfway through Vermont: White River Village.

Construction began in 1846 after a ground breaking ceremony in Windsor. The first tracks through White River Village were put down near Nutt Lane. From there the lines grew north through the neighboring village of Hartford, pushing forty feet of rail at a time through valleys and over rivers, northwest through Sharon, Royalton, Bethel, towards the capital in Montpelier. The line grew south towards Windsor more slowly, then along a prescribed track through part of New Hampshire before coming back across the river at Bellows Falls. Every year brought ten or twelve miles of fresh track, the clearing crews working to open the forests for the leveling crews, who built right-of-ways for the track laying crews, who settled stout, square timbers firmly into the soil and fastened across their coarse backs the steel rails of progress.

Comprised largely of immigrants, these crews faced difficult working conditions in the best of weather, and incredible discomfort when the short summers turned into chilly autumns. Production continued as long, and started as early, as nature allowed.

The work was hard and dangerous, but especially so for Phineas Gage. Born in Lebanon, New Hampshire—across the Connecticut from White River Junction—he contributed to both the Vermont railroad and medical science. In 1848 he was working near Cavendish, tamping gunpowder into a hole to blast some rocks out of the rail bed. No one poured sand on top of the powder, as was customary, so sparks made by his steel tamping rod ignited it. The three foot long rod shot out of the hole and completely through his head, pinning man and legacy into the medical record books; he lived, but wasn't quite the same person anymore. His accident was not without precedent, but his recovery—and the change in his personality—was so remarkable that he has a permanent place in modern psychology: the man who lost his frontal lobes, and then ran away to drive a stagecoach in Chile.

Though it nearly killed Phineas, the difficult work brought welcome opportunities for thousands of men… and not only Vermonters. Howard Logan, the Boston and Maine mechanic I met, told me all about the men who laid the tracks. They were old men when he was a boy, but he knew them; as a man, he worked the lines they built so long ago. The history and lore got into his blood, making him a true Yankee railroad man.

"A lot of Italians were hired to build the railroads," he said. "Some of the immigrants would sneak into the country and work for nothing, 'cause that was more than they had back home. That was the kind of help they could get. They appreciated an opportunity, and grabbed a hold of it and worked their butts off." They built the future as they laid the tracks, constructing new lives for themselves while opening a new world for native Vermonters. When railroad work ran out, some moved on and others stayed, as happens when any major industry shifts. Those who remained found other jobs, establishing their ties to the community. "They grew up through the years," Howard said. "They were police chiefs and lawyers, and everything else."

Everything else, like cooks on the rail crews, grocery store owners and restaurateurs. I smell bread baking at C&S Pizza, just a block away on South Main Street, and for a moment I wonder if Chris would like to catch a very early lunch. He stands on the platform, pouring over the timetable he maintains. Amtrak trains pause to board passengers who pre-purchased their tickets online; the ticket window in a little anteroom just off the platform is covered over from the inside, and hasn't been manned in years. Trains don't generally stop here any longer. As honorary historian, Chris keeps these records—what time the trains roll through, the type and number of locomotives, how many cars they pull—largely for himself.

These trains don't interest me much. The locomotives are yellow and dingy, burning diesel fuel instead of coal, and pull rusted steel cars in mile long, repetitive trains; but he loves them. I'm more interested in the steam engines, that romantic notion of a coal-black locomotive pulling a train *clackity-clackity-clack* through the mountains with a *hoo-hoo* whistle and bright red boxcars. He shows me the hand-marked timetables for this week's trains; I explain how I was just thinking about the *very* first ones.

The very first one, he said, was the Abigail Adams: a wood burning steam locomotive that followed the workers along the rails as they laid them. That big, black engine "built the railroad," Chris says. She pulled cars loaded with picks, shovels, adzes, ties, spikes, tracks... everything the workers needed that they couldn't fashion onsite. While she crawled the tracks with supplies, working with the men out there in the wilderness, a different engine claimed the glory for opening the line.

Passengers climbed aboard the first commercial run on Monday morning, June 26th, 1848, for a ride northwest to Bethel. Pulled by the steam engine named Winooski, those first passengers rode for twenty-five miles, stepping onto the platform and into the annals of history. Two weeks later, on Monday, July 10th, the first freight train pulled out of White River Junction. Some consider the official opening of the Central Vermont Railroad services to have come on June 20th, 1849, with the inaugural trip from White River Junction all the way to the state capital in Montpelier. The Governor himself greeted that train. Each year the tracks connected new mountain hamlets, opening them to travel and trade and changing many in the same ways they changed White River Junction. "Everything went in increments," I remember Howard saying about the steady progress, "just like the roads: another fourteen miles, another ten miles, and then there'd be big celebrations." Those were the days of brass bands and governors kissing babies. The railroad was coming to town—celebrate! And celebrate they did, all throughout Vermont; all throughout the latter 1800s.

White River Junction, at the intersection of two rivers, two eras, two rail lines, and growing daily, needed a station. The Connecticut River Railroad Company, just *after* rail service began, bought land between the tracks and the river. They signed the deed on September 8th, 1848, and began construction by importing sand in great quantities—their deed bought several acres of swampland. Construction followed the designs of Ammi B. Young, a celebrated architect born across the river in Phineas Gage's old hometown. If you ever noticed how the Boston Customs House, Montpelier capital building, two Dartmouth College buildings, and the original White River Union Station kind of look like cousins, that's why—same guy. Young pioneered the use of iron extensively in construction, and he used local materials—such as Barre granite in the Montpelier capitol—to create classic Italianate and Revival details.

Even if you haven't seen Young's buildings, you probably have seen his work: the US Treasury Department's symbol of a fist holding a key. Now consider that he was hired to design the train station in a small village in the Green Mountains, and you see the importance the state of Vermont placed on their railroad.

Everything about the early railroad was grand, from the sheer size of the steel locomotives and the cars they towed to the clacks and roars they made steaming down the tracks. Locomotives stood taller than people, the size of some buildings, crossing ties it took two men to lift. Canoes, small barges, and later riverboats (on the southern stretches of the Connecticut) moved loads downriver; horses towed buggies and coaches; but then came these trains that moved wood and steel boxcars the size of cabins. The unprecedented sight was over-whelming, as if the very future itself were lumbering up the rails with a brave new world in tow. Bring on the brass bands, indeed, and a grand station to welcome the future.

The first locomotives were steel and iron with brass pipes connecting to glass-face gauges in the engineer's compartment. Two iron wheels aligned the locomotive's front end with the track, while pairs of larger wheels provided the tractive power. The engineer's compartment behind the giant boiler housed the three man crew: engineer, fireman, and brakeman. Following close behind was the tender car—it tended the locomotive—a box on wheels carrying the fuel (wood at first; later, coal) for the engine, and hundreds of gallons of additional water for the boiler. Engines were designated by their number of wheels and where they were arranged—like the popular 2-8-4 configuration: two wheels guided the locomotive, eight wheels pulled with the power of more than a thousand horses, and four wheels rolled under the tender.

Each of the three men performed an essential job: the engineer controlled the speed, slowing for turns and bridges, speeding up for hills, and gauging the distance they would coast when pulling into a station. "It was a tough job to be an engineer," Howard explained, reflecting on the glory days. "When you brought back that throttle, if you give it just a little too much when she's really, really pulling, those wheels would spin like a son of a gun. That wasn't good on the tires, steel on steel. Those engines were so huge, if he slipped 'em, it would shake the hell out of the whole locomotive. It would shake the firebox up too, which is a huge, huge, firebox, so the fireman would have to contend with that thing and rebuild it."

The brakeman operated the lone brake—a friction pad under the tender that he engaged by spinning a wheel. If having only one brake on a big train seems dangerous, consider being a brakeman tending friction pads on many different cars in later train designs. That job was the most dangerous on the crew. "As you go back on the cars," Chris explains, "there was a leaf thing. They had a brakeman who would run down the whole train setting brakes, and it was very dangerous." The cars lurched and bounded over the tracks at great rates of speed, making balance difficult and scampering from car to car across their roofs rather harrowing. Many brakemen slipped once; virtually no one lived to slip again.

The fireman had the most physically demanding vocation, as he shoveled fuel into the firebox beneath the boiler. There was only one fireman per train, and for the duration of the trip—from three to twenty-five miles—he would run between the firebox and the tender car with shovelfuls of fuel, heaving them into the firebox to spread the coals evenly under the long boiler. "That fireman," Howard explained, "he'd work his ass off. They had to have the steam up there all the time, up to one-hundred-eighty to two-hundred-thirty pounds per square inch."

The Connecticut River Railroad Company laid several rail yards—sections of track where trains pulled off the main route while others used the line. Maintenance crews serviced and repaired the cars during this down time, their engineers, brakemen and firemen retreating to quarters in the station or hotels nearby. Trains did not run at night until the late 1800s, by virtue of the danger involved in running through darkness. Oil-burning headlamps could only cast beams seventy-five to a hundred feet forward, and signal flags were off to the sides of the track—frequently in night-shadows.

Missing an important signal—such as a "bridge out" flag—would be disastrous. It takes hundreds of yards to stop a steam powered train (a few miles to stop a modern one), and distance was not a luxury the engineers could afford should things go wrong in the dark.

With travelers and crews needing lodging each evening, and thru-passengers needing layover accommodations, there was a ready need for an inn near every station. Colonel Sam Nutt, a riverboat captain, purchased the Grafton House hotel in Enfield, New Hampshire, had it moved twenty miles, and reassembled it across the tracks from the new station in White River Village. Renamed the Junction House, it opened with fanfare and instant success.

But for all that the railroad changed travel, its freight service had the greatest impact on White River Village. "We are apt to think of the benefit we derive from the railroads in terms of convenience and comfort in personal travel," Hopkins said in that 1938 speech, "but in the large the major benefit to us is in the economical transportation of foodstuffs, of fuel, and of the multitude of staples of daily life to which we have become so accustomed that we hold them indispensable to daily existence. In 1930 the passenger revenues of American railroads was $731,000,000, while their income from freight was $4,145,000,000." Consider 1930's prices—you could buy a new house for only $7,000. In dollar terms, the railroads made enough money from freight services alone to buy 592,143 houses…in one year. That's five and a half times as much money as they made from passenger tickets.

Horse drawn, overland shipping was slow, dangerous, and extremely expensive—and the distribution of

12

perishable goods, even moderately perishable goods like crackers, was confined to small territories. Direct, quick, and comparably inexpensive rail lines connecting suppliers with new markets created fresh sales territory, and lower cost access to materials. Bakers and manufacturers could import ingredients and parts, rather than suffer the limitations of local production. This facilitated job specialization—for example, one mill on a large river could produce more lumber than their local market demanded, sending the excess to market inland…rather than letting excess logs float to competitors downstream. The finished products—from foodstuffs to furniture, livestock to textiles—could be distributed to diverse and disperse markets. Viva la transportation revolución, indeed.

Pre-railroad, it cost a hundred dollars to send a ton of goods overland from Buffalo, New York, to Albany. Compare that with this railroad rate from 1937: a penny per ton, per mile, on the Boston and Maine Railroad… just under three dollars to ship the same goods an equal distance. The economy boomed, and White River Village lined its rail yards with warehouses, factories, and bakeries; the rush was on for city jobs as the railroad came into its glory days.

These new businesses thrived on shipping, with warehouses in the Gates Block across Main Street and all along the tracks; the Junction House filled its rooms as fast as passenger cars unloaded. Homes and tenements rose in the open spaces, and the town welcomed shops of the sort required to clothe and feed its growing population. People came in from the farmland, the outlying communities, and even from Hartford, the town just across the White River. I ask Chris about this, and he looks up the rails towards the northbound bridge.

"The 1850s is when everything kind of moved down here," he says. Though today Hartford has more businesses than the quiet White River Junction, the rail yards—and jobs—were south of the bridge. It makes sense that an economic boom that attracted workers for hundreds of miles would also pull them from just half a mile away, but it still strikes me funny how folks living so close would move—actually *move*—half a mile.

The businesses had to, though, and where the job goes, so too go the workers. There were no cars in the latter 1800s, meaning no delivery trucks to haul flour and lard even a short distance from the rail yards to the warehouse. They built along the tracks instead, so men with hand trucks could wheel boxes and crates directly in and out of the cars from their loading dock. It was a good time to own land in White River Village. They were in the midst of a bold new era, and about to change their name to keep up with the times.

"On the map of 1869," Chris says, "it was known as White River Village. Then you have White River, which is how it appeared on some of the schedules," up until the late 1800's. It's been White River Junction ever since. What's in a name? They were a village at a river junction before the railroad. Then the tracks made White River the junction of two rail lines, and the junction where farm met town—so many junctions all in one place, with more to come in time.

Dry goods and sundries came in, making their way to the farmers and loggers who sent their produce and timber out on the next train. Their previous era, of quiet Green Mountain seclusion, log drives, and scattered river traffic, came to an end; locomotives pulled into

14

the junction with the steam age in tow, and everything changed—even their name.

* * * * *

Promontory Summit, Utah, May 10, 1869: the day Vermont linked up with California. Sort of. From Vermont, a series of rail connections led all the way to New York City. From there, trains could travel across the vast North American interior all the way to California. Should fortune favor their whims, folks who never expected to leave Vermont could arrive on the other side of the continent in about a week.

There was new fuel in the fireboxes: coal. Though it produced more soot than wood, it also burned hotter, meaning that less fuel by weight could propel the trains farther. As metallurgy improved, the hotter burning coal increased boiler pressures to produce even more power. With the new fuel, trains picked up speed and range as they clacked and chugged over the Passumpsic lines north to Montpelier, or south to Windsor and Bellows Falls.

The railroad appealed to Everett Smith, who decided to relocate his family's bakery from Hanover, New Hampshire—five miles upriver—to the edge of the rail yard in White River Junction. Their bakery produced the Hanover Cracker, created in 1815 by the Symnes family.

The Smiths bought the Symnes's bakery in 1837, continuing production and local delivery by horse drawn wagon. That was the past—a successful one, no doubt—but Everett saw the future in lower ingredient costs, greater market access, and a bigger facility. He moved

E.K. Smith & Sons to the northern end of Railroad Row in 1871, into a brand new brick building. The trains in the North Yard rested mere feet from his loading dock, bringing fresh flour, sugar, and lard from points throughout New England. The boxcars rolled away with barrels of Hanover Crackers—record numbers of them.

A decade later Everett joined Alma and S.L. Farman in a new venture, the White River Paper Company—one of several businesses in his growing empire. He exported confections and paper throughout New England, and capitalized on the growing local population by serving their needs as well. The Smiths built tenement houses, established the First National Bank of White River, built a school, and even built the Evangelical Church, all to serve the townspeople who worked for him in increasing numbers and ways. More than three hundred workers staffed the Smith & Sons bakery alone; their jobs all dependent upon the railroad.

The main line connected with spurs leading to smaller towns, including the Woodstock Railway that laid tracks despite opposition from the Central Vermont Railroad Company. The first Woodstock Railway train rolled in 1875, the year they built a station to welcome the same commercial boom that built White River Junction. The stationmaster welcomed the locomotive, standing at the leading edge of his platform to greet the future. In other towns along the rails, stationmasters gave one of two signals: an open-palm wave called a "flag stop," meaning that the train should make a stop, or the closed-fist "highball," meaning to keep on going. They didn't need to do that in Woodstock, as their station was at the end of the line...and so was the economic boom they expected—it never really happened...at least, not on

White River Junction's scale, which in light of future events may have been a saving grace.

More than fifty trains a day pulled through White River Junction. Most of their cars were boxcars and flatbeds for cargo and timber, but many of the trains had a few passenger cars as well. Businessmen and diplomats rode these cars between Montpelier and points south, even as far as Boston and New York. If you imagine their ride as a scenic tour of lush forests in the Green Mountains, consider this: the forests were clear cut, the trees milled into lumber for buildings, bridges, and railroad ties, with the excess sold to booming construction markets down the line.

The early locomotives burned wood—a lot of it— rather than coal, and even after the switch, wood was a popular heat source for homes and businesses during the long New England winters. The verdant Vermont forests we know today grew since that era; they were decimated in the name of progress during those glory days of the railroad. Passengers certainly had spectacular views of the Connecticut River and rolling countryside, but it was not quite the verdant woodland crossing you might imagine.

Chris tells me how the forests were ravaged for decades, and even now—when so much of Vermont is postcard-ready—the forests still haven't fully recovered. "The forestation of this area is only about eighty percent of the way back to where it once was," he says. "It was deforested completely for the railroad." Most of the passengers were businessmen and statesmen, though, not ecologists; their concern was the railroad's economic impact...not their ecological footprint. Vast fields of weeds and rotting stumps were mere side effects, like how the rivers turned reddish-brown for some reason downstream from the mills. These images are abhorrent today, in an era of "green" technology and "carbon footprints," but such concepts didn't exist back then; science, at that point, couldn't measure the environmental impact, and very few people seemed interested anyway. Forests were lumber and fuel sources, and that was that.

They still haven't entirely recovered.

* * * * *

Most of the trains through White River Junction were freightliners, and their most important cargo, Chris says, was coal—it fueled the trains, heated many homes, and boiled water for many steam-powered machines used in manufacturing. Lumber and granite from Barre quarries rolled south, and animals also rode the rails—alive, as well as in the form of cars full of hides destined for shoe factories and tanneries. One tannery, across the Connecticut River in Lebanon, brought a good amount of animal products through White River Junction; it formerly stood on the banks of a creek across the street from my old apartment, my home being on the top floor of a tenement house the tannery owned—I can trace the existence of my old home, among far more notable buildings, right back to the effect of the railroad.

Textiles rolled through White River Junction as well, coming from mills along the rivers and streams, heading to factories down south in Boston. The Smith & Sons Bakery pumped lard straight from container cars into storage vats through pipes in the walls of their bakery. The crews at Union Station kept things running, if not always smoothly, then at least on time. Occasionally, though, disaster struck…and there was no more disaster prone building than Union Station.

Consider the buildings in that period: wooden structures with papered walls, hardwood floors, and no synthetic coatings, finishes, or furnishings. Much of the wood was treated in flammable preservatives to keep from rotting. All paperwork was actual paper, in overstuffed cabinets and drawers. At night, everything was illuminated with gas or oil flames, and in winter, everything was heated with wood or coal. Fires were fierce, frequent, and reshaped many towns.

Fire consumed most of the Junction House in 1878; at that time it was owned by the Barrons family, who purchased it some nineteen years earlier. The fire came as no surprise to certain community members, as it was "regarded as 'the natural sequence of the unrestricted looseness that characterized his (the senior proprietor's) system of running the Public House,'" according to an anonymous history of the hotel provided by its modern proprietors. Seems that in an era where "loose morals" could bring about a person's "downfall," a devastating fire seems the natural consequence of a laissez-faire business philosophy at a public house. Today we might write about such a fire in terms of liability and insurance; that author seemed to revel in the fire and brimstone. Times have certainly changed.

The Junction House was quickly rebuilt, and bigger—the new incarnation had more than two hundred rooms. Soon thereafter, Ballard and Andrews purchased the business and transformed its reputation into one of a stately and proper hotel.

Fire destroyed the train station in 1881 for the

first of many times. It was rebuilt, and rail business continued expanding, improving, and changing. In the latter 1800s, the Boston & Maine Railroad purchased the Passumpsic lines northbound from the station, as well as the Connecticut River Railroad Company lines to the south. A round trip to Woodstock in 1885, via the Woodstock Railway from White River Junction, cost passengers one dollar. Fare to Quechee, round trip, cost only sixty cents, or forty cents for a one-way ticket. Despite the fires, business grew at a steady pace as the Connecticut Valley closed in on the end of a dynamic century.

The twentieth century began with the clang of fire bells, as in 1908 the station burned for a second time. Promptly rebuilt again, it was back in service by 1909.

Farther down the yard, south towards Windsor, was an impressive twenty-three stall roundhouse. Locomotives that needed repair drove onto a giant wood and steel turntable that rotated them to face tracks leading into one of the many stalls. They rolled backwards into their stall, the workers turned the table to align with another stall, and a replacement engine pulled into the yard.

Mechanic teams replaced worn parts and oiled the many steel joints. "They had to grease those rods by hand, with grease guns," Howard explained. His job with the B&M included grease gun duty. "There was an awful lot of maintenance," he said, almost wistfully— many years retired, it was still obvious how much he loved the railroad. Perhaps a bit of distance from those days oiling and fixing locomotives helped him forget the aches and recall the joys more fondly.

Scores of mechanics kept the trains rolling, as business boomed through the first ten years of the new

20

century…despite another interruption: to rebuild the station after it was destroyed by fire again in 1911, its third time being reduced to smoldering rubble.

Rail traffic increased even more in 1917, after the April 6th declaration of war on Germany. Wood, wool, war materials and soldiers rolled south to the port cities.

From the earliest days of their passenger service, the trains brought students and visitors through White River Junction and up to Norwich—right across the river from Dartmouth College. The college relied heavily on the Boston & Maine for passenger service to and from their remote campus, as the railroad was the most effective way to traverse northern New England. I mentioned that a while back to Bill Brighman, a member of the Board of Directors for the New England Transportation Institute and Museum, and former stationmaster for White River Junction. "Back in 1900, 1910," he said, "there was no other transportation to compete with it. There had to be at least thirty passenger trains every day."

Formerly, people rode horse drawn coaches up the frozen Connecticut River in the winter, or made their way slowly overland in warmer months; nothing competed with the speed, ease, and cost of the new rail service. Travel back then was mostly undertaken out of necessity; students arriving at Dartmouth by train usually did not depart again until after they graduated. When they were ready to reenter the world, those who chose to leave the Upper Valley did so upon one of the countless trains bound south through White River Junction.

The initial, explosive expansion of rail lines and service matured in the first ten years of the new century, as the initial rush of booming business tapered into more stable growth. Established stops along the lines grew in influence to the point where new towns added to a rail line were challenged to compete with established destinations. This competition took hold among rail town businesses the country over, and though they were largely doing well, the early days of unchecked growth and ad-hoc monopoly were over. Things might have calmed down, with populations, prices, and shipping routes stabilizing, but then World War I broke out.

U.S. involvement demanded supplies and soldiers be shipped from all parts of the country to the eastern seaboard. Resources were hauled from mines and forests to factories and made into equipment, before being loaded on trains again to meet ships bound for Europe. Thus, the natural post-new-technology boom didn't slow down like it otherwise would have. The very real opportunities, along with decades of then-familiar growth, created a false sense of security. Swollen with workers and relying on large volumes of business sent along the rails, White River Junction was set up for a mighty fall...and America was set up for the Great Depression.

World War I ended in 1918, its wave of war-commerce-prosperity still rolling across the country on the railways. Soldiers rejoined the workforce and engineering turned once again to civil matters—with new ideas and technology developed during the war. The next generation of steam engines debuted, and the roundhouse at the White River Junction station underwent renovations to accommodate the new, larger 2-10-4 locomotives. Robert Jones wrote in <u>Central Vermont Railway, A Yankee Tradition</u>, "The big engine-house at White River Junction underwent extensive repairs, and four of the stalls were extended to accommodate the larger locomotives." The roundhouse welcomed these steam monsters among their other locomotives.

Chris calls them "700s," and likened their power to a more recent locomotive: the Challenger. On this platform here, decades removed from the reign of those iron giants, Chris closes his eyes and loses himself in their grandeur. "The Challenger engine, your Big Boys, were the only trains in the country that could pull a five-and-a-half mile train with no help," he says. The he mutters something about 40,000 horsepower coming from a single engine, and how they hauled the longest trains over the steepest grades in the Green Mountains.

They stayed in Vermont, though, as many trestles were built only for their lighter predecessors; the 700s were too heavy to safely leave the state. "Vermont is known as a cornucopia of engines," Chris continues, eyes open again and scanning the empty tracks. "We've had everything in the state around this station: Altos, forty-four tonners, SW1200s, SW100s, RSDs, you name it, it's probably been here. But two-ten-fours, they were the biggest that ran through." Big and small, they kept White River Junction lively as the years closed in on the Great Depression.

* * * * *

Colonel Wheeler purchased the Junction House hotel in the early '20s, renaming it in 1924 for his frequent customer John Calvin Coolidge, the father of Calvin Coolidge—the thirtieth President of the United States. Maybe it didn't like its new name—a year later the hotel burned down…again.

After decades of growth and success, the spirit of the age was one of hope and development; even as the over-inflated city neared its collapse, Wheeler rebuilt the hotel and continued its dignified service under the name, Hotel Coolidge, it still bears today.

The 1920s do not look so rosy in hindsight as they may have seemed at the time. The "War to End All Wars" was over and its economic boom still lingered, but the decade was sandwiched between an unprecedented war and an unprecedented depression. According to Economics professor Robert Schenk of St. Joseph's College, between 1925 and 1929 (six to ten years after WWI ended), 104 of every 10,000 American businesses failed—compared with 23 per 10,000 in the 1940s.

The first decades of open rail traffic saw business flourish from new connections to previously untapped suppliers and markets. Small communities across America changed as businesses sprang up in railroad towns, which grew exponentially from the influx of workers, money, and the businesses that support expanding communities. This redefined small-town urban living in White River Junction, and throughout America.

* * * * *

The United States economy fell into crippling economic recession in August of 1929, two months before the Black Thursday stock market crash on October 24th. The ensuing Great Depression broke many small businesses, and pruned the ambitions and developments of many large ones as well. Rail service continued, but with widespread fear and lack of surplus capital, the boom went bust and left many businesses barely scraping by. The Smith & Son bakery folded in 1934. Other businesses dried up as well, and the national unemployment trend fell hard on the working class population. Last week I spoke with Mike Farnsworth, the veteran B&M yardman and clerk, about his Great Depression days.

"We lived beside the railway when I was a kid," he recalled with a survivor's smile, "over there in West Lebanon. For fourteen years we never burned anything but the coal I picked up in the yard. Every night after school I had to go pick up two pails of coal. Sometimes in the winter time they'd shovel it right off into my pail." Howard Logan then added, "You'd scrounge the whole yard just to find a piece of coal."

Howard recalled the lengths people, often transient for lack of money to settle in any one place, would go to for food. "Those were depression days, I'll tell you, you didn't have any money, you were just poor. Back in those days, there used to be hobos, people who were homeless, and they would run the rails, and they would come into White River here looking for work and food, knocking on doors. Some of the widows, ya know, would have them saw up the driftwood for winter. So, they would go down on the Connecticut River and catch all the driftwood and haul it home. They had big sheds, and that's all they had to keep warm. They didn't waste it, either."

The citizens held on to what they had, working towards brighter days that seemed impossibly far off. In 1935 the fire bells announced a structure fire as the train station burned for the fourth time in eighty-seven years.

Reconstructing it provided jobs for otherwise unemployed workers, the effort culminating in the fifth and current version of the station. On December 8th, 1937, Dartmouth College president Ernest Martin Hopkins gave an abbreviated speech dedicating the new station, while behind him the Dartmouth College Band experienced instrument failure in the freezing cold.

The January, 1938 Dartmouth Alumni Magazine reported another instance of bumbled ceremony at the dedication when Captain-elect Bob MacLeod "attempt(ed) to kick into the river a football to which a key was attached to indicate that the station would never be locked. Bob's kick barely cleared the head of an encircling crowd of kids, traveled a short distance through the air, and fell about 20 yards short of the river bank where an over-confident group of supporters was awaiting the arrival of the ball."

I mention this to Chris, here on the platform next to the building that ceremony dedicated. Chris suggests that despite the station's misfortunes, something must have worked: the station has not burned down since.

* * * * *

The military-industrial buildup for World War II, among other factors, helped end the Great Depression. Vast unemployment and poverty relief measures pulled the country up by its bootstraps, and though few new businesses opened among the shuttered warehouses in White River Junction, at least the crushing poverty abated slightly when rail traffic picked back up. White River Junction's doom was through the door, though, making itself a sandwich and getting comfortable for a long stay.

The war brought a boom in freight transport, from which the local lines made a few cents per "ton mile" for use of the tracks; businesses moved relevant goods, and the military transport trains made quite an impression on the town. Farnsworth told me about the tight security on a 105-car train carrying war materials southbound. "We weren't allowed to get near it!" he said, adding that its "head was in New Hampshire, the tail was in Vermont!" Military detachments guarded railroad trestles throughout New England, and mentioning this to Chris, he tells me how an anti-aircraft battery was erected for the defense of White River Junction's rail yards in case of aerial attack. The Nazis never attacked Vermont, but according to Howard, the railroad companies were billed for the protection services along their lines anyway.

Having such a military presence in rural Vermont—the rumored antiaircraft battery, guards at the trestles, mysterious trains well-guarded in the yards—seems strange, and even those who tell me about it do so with a wry grin. But the early 1940s paranoia about the Nazis was no less terrifying—or motivating—than our fear of terrorists was in late 2001. We got the TSA and the Patriot Act; all the rail companies got was a bill for some seriously bored soldiers. Anyway...

Labor force dynamics changed remarkably after World War II, and America embraced the transportation revolution enabled by President Roosevelt's "New Deal." Among other departments and initiatives, Roosevelt created the Civil Works Administration (CWA) that provided construction-related jobs to ease unemployment; they used their funding and workforce to build highways across the United States. Henry Ford's inventions had caught on, and Roosevelt thought a vast highway system for private automobiles would benefit America. At least, building them would create millions of jobs. The CWA also repaired existing roads, preparing them for vehicular use. This paved the way for President Eisenhower's initiative in the 1950s to connect the country with thousands of miles of interstate highways. Nearly a hundred years prior a vast, interconnected (rail)road system revolutionized America; another one was on the way...but this time, for personal automobiles and shipping trucks.

Building upon the CWA's progress, the interstate boom facilitated the mass personal transit that, in turn, necessitated the interstates themselves. Local delivery trucks made longer trips, and vehicle engines and frames grew stronger, carrying heavier loads much farther distances. Reliable delivery vehicles on greatly improved roads enabled businesses to establish themselves farther and farther away from railroad centers, without prohibitive increases in shipping costs or hassles. With the highway system, trucks came to play a major role in all levels of the shipping process, increasingly cutting rail transportation out of the picture. Delivery trucks picked up produce from farms, dropped it off at loading docks on the rail lines, and then drove past rows of empty warehouses on their way back to the garage.

For cargo with low value-to-volume ratios, like the tons of coal moved in railcar hoppers, trains were still the best bet. But businesses increasingly turned to trucks for their distribution needs. The result was the economic decentralization of Railroad Rows across the country…and another blow to downtown White River Junction. Many remaining businesses moved out of the city centers, out among their customers and away from high-rent railroad frontage land, none the worse because their trucks kept them connected to associated businesses and railways.

The New Deal also created the National Labor Relations Act, which laid the legal rails for the unionization of the railroad. Labor unions formed in White River Junction and all over America, incorporated for the mutual defense of workers against layoffs and pay cuts such as they suffered during the Great Depression. More than seventy years since unionization, many union workers adore the institution…but everyone supports it. Mike and Howard still bristle at their mention.

"They had one for everyone," Howard told me gravely. "It was pathetic. That's why we don't work for the railroads anymore. That's why a lot of our mills aren't here anymore, because of the unions." The railroads, under pressure to cut costs from the declining income in their passenger and freight services, had to cut their spending without altering their payouts to employees. The National Labor Relations Act prohibited union-busting, putting the Boston and Maine and Central Vermont companies at their mercy. So too, then, were the employees themselves.

"Then they became so compartmentalized," Howard said, "that if you were a laborer, you only did certain types of work, and anyone caught doing laborer's work that wasn't theirs, they'd time slip him. Four hours they had to pay for that violation." He gave an example of oil spilling on a platform. Only the laborers were allowed to clean the oil up, and if anyone else—such as an engineer or clerk—so much as threw rags on the oil to keep their shoes from getting messy, they could be fined four hours' pay, he said. "That's what they were doing to the railroads," he opined. "If you were a real railroader, you felt bad about how the railroads were treated."

Automobiles allowed towns to develop in far-flung areas—supplies came to them in trucks, and workers could commute to or from outlying districts. With consumers living in one area and working in another, there were new opportunities for point-of-sale businesses in their neighborhoods. Train stations became pickup and departure points rather than destinations, and the businesses that catered to them competed fiercely in the few minutes before the cars picked the passengers up and whisked them away. The old downtown focus, of hotels and restaurants within walking distance, disappeared as the businesses sought customers elsewhere.

This happened throughout America just as it did in White River Junction. Businesses distanced themselves economically and physically from the stations. Towns expanded on the automobile scale, rather than the pedestrian scale, as private vehicles became practical for in-town transportation. Travelers might as well drive their cars to visit other cities, which the improved vehicles and highways allowed like never before. With increasingly decentralized city layouts, travelers needed personal transportation once they arrived there anyway.

Consider Europe, with its narrow streets and economies ravaged by two consecutive world wars. European cities didn't see so much of the personal car craze in the mid-1900s. They rebuilt and expanded their rail lines and developed public transportation apace the new technology. Rather than allocating time and reconstruction resources on urban sprawl, they spent the mid century rebuilding their cities on essentially the same layouts—thus explaining, in some small part, why European mass transit is generally better than you find in most American cities. Part of it has to do with how they revamped their mass transit infrastructure during reconstruction, when cities could afford buses but citizens couldn't afford cars; meanwhile, Americans were in lust with our personal cars and the freedom of rolling them along the expansive new highways...and soldiers returning from the war had the cash to buy them.

Phoenix, Arizona, provides a parallel example of what happened in America just after World War II. In the late 1880s they gained railroad access (replacing actual wagon trains), enabling the tiny desert outpost to receive the food and supplies needed to support people and the business ventures they started—a bit like an arid version of the White River Junction story. Military bases and industries, receiving food and materials via the railroads, brought businesses and workers to the desert. Then the highway system, post WWII personal wealth, and the family car decentralized the city and sent it sprawling across the desert. It turned from a town with a few stoplights before WWII, into a city of millions in just a few decades—a boom like the one the railroads first brought to White River Junction. But after the war, their fates diverged.

By 2007, 4.2 million people lived in 517 square miles worth of Phoenix—around 3,000 people per square mile. Paris, at the time, packed around 64,000 people per square mile...the automobile size city vs. the pedestrian size city. White River Junction was built on the pedestrian scale, like Paris and other European cities, and on that scale the railroad-centered downtown businesses thrived; then Eisenhower's interstates hemmed them in on the south and west, bringing the automobile era and a whole new epoch.

Many towns that could decentralize and sprawl, did. In White River Junction, motels went in along the highways on the outskirts of town, out in the cheap land on the periphery. Phoenix sprawled from the influence of the same technology and wealth; White River Junction, hemmed in to the north by the White River, the east by the Connecticut River, the west and south by the interstate, and all around by the Green Mountains, had nowhere to sprawl.

After nearly a century of public rail transport, the next neat, new thing was owning your own car and reveling in the pure American freedom of the open road—for travel and day-to-day transportation, and moving your business away from commercial areas and out into communities. Our personal territories expanded. Let grandpa take the train; we have a car.

The glory days of the railroad were over.

* * * * *

Passenger traffic on the trains dwindled, even as personal finances returned to comfortable levels post-Great Depression. Though families and business travelers could afford to take the trains again, the highways, city layouts, and convenience of traveling in the family car made rail service feel outdated. As the calendars neared 1950, the primary passenger services through White River Junction had truncated to just local trains running a hundred twenty miles to St. Albans. The era of mass passenger travel ended not with a bang, but a whimper.

Another era drew to a close as well. The diesel engines developed for ship use were configured for rail power, and a new locomotive chugged onto the scene: the diesel-powered FM units, freight locomotives with sleek, futuristic looks. They were lower maintenance, generally more powerful, and required one less trained crewman than steam engines—with liquid fuel pumped automatically through the engine, there was no need for a fireman.

"When they went into diesel, there wasn't anything for the fireman to do but sit there," Howard explained. Yet the unions refused to allow the B&M and other lines to eliminate the position, he said—they insisted that every diesel engine be staffed with the same complement of three as in the steam engine days. "He wasn't doing a damn thing but riding," Howard continued, exasperated again. "They called it 'featherbedding.' They tried and tried and tried to get rid of that third man in the cab, and couldn't." Some traditions die hard, for reasons altogether their own.

Dieselization—the official term for the conversion from coal to diesel fuel—was completed in 1957, when the Central Vermont wheeled their last nineteen steam engines into retirement. The last mainline steam run on the northern lines was made by Engine 602, a 4-8-2 locomotive bound on April 4th from White River Junction north to St. Albans. Two days later the last revenue generating run by a steam engine—Engine 466—rolled over the Richford Branch, bound as well for St. Albans. The Boston & Maine ceased their passenger runs north in 1962. On September 3, 1966, the Interstate Commerce Commission authorized the B&M to cease all passenger transportation south to Springfield, Massachusetts. No brass band bid adieu to the passenger cars. No one fished a key out of the river to symbolically lock the station doors.

Robert Jones wrote, "This development spelled 'finis' to the CV's last remaining passenger trains operating between Montreal and White River Junction... On the final trip of the 'Washingtonian,' there were only nine passengers aboard. Not only was there now no passenger service on the Central Vermont, there was no such service anywhere else in the state."

When he began work with the B&M, Mike was one of about four hundred employees at White River Station. "When I quit," he said, "there was one man, and that was me." Other major employers folded, the town slowly imploding. The familiar role of the railroad as employer, shipper, and lifeline all but disappeared. The end of steam engines, passenger service, rail-based business, and the glory days of the railroad fell heavily upon White River Junction.

Fewer and fewer trains stopped in town. Those rolling past came up from the south with loads of salt and malt and fuel oil, or down from Montpelier and Barre with lumber and granite, rolling slowly through the quiet remains of the once-bustling town. When someone mounted the Union Station platform, it was to give the highball sign and raise their clench fists against the dying of an era.

* * * * *

Chris and I leave that platform, walking north along a sidewalk towards a stately black locomotive lovingly preserved in thick black rust-proof paint. Its name, 494, is painted in proud numbers on the front of her boiler. She sits under a roof, and you can touch her giant wheels and climb into the engineer's compartment. Our conversation winds down as we stand here on the crew deck. She faces north, towards Barre, Montpelier, and Canada, once the direction of the railroad's future. Chris stares vacantly at the smokestack, gathering his thoughts. He's talked me through the railroad's history, and here we are in the present, a quiet moment beside empty tracks. "We have thirteen trains a day through here," he explains; one just about every two hours. "Two of 'em are local 600s, which are now daylights. They run between here and Bellows Falls." He found some hope to hold onto, and though the preceding seems an elegy, he clings to it.

Chris knows so much about the railroad because he loves it; he talked my ear off this morning, hoping to instill in me the sort of passion for locomotives and railroad history that fuels his volunteerism, entertains him, stokes his imagination. The joy is coming back in his voice now, and he speaks a bit more rapidly.

"Sometimes they'll make a rare move to Mt. Peculiar. The two freighters are 324 South and 323 North. They only go as far as Brattleboro." When the cars rumble through, they pass this station at fifteen miles an hour before speeding up again to forty, then fifty on the straightaway. The cargoes here in the early years of the twenty first century are timber, plastics, heating oil, propane, and salt. Malt passes through on its way to animal feed centers and breweries. Coal rolls

35

by in dirty hoppers, bound for out-of-state markets.

The lone passenger service through White River Junction, save weekend-only excursion rides north along the Connecticut River past the Montshire Museum, is the daily Amtrak service with the silver cars that lost their luster years ago. They run two cars, one southbound, one northbound, on the B&M tracks through White River Junction on their daily run from St. Albans to Washington, DC. The two trains pass each other somewhere between Hartford, Connecticut, and Springfield, Massachusetts. The amenities inside are pleasant, and their luggage restrictions and security are far more traveler-friendly than airlines—yet the bulk of their seats are empty.

The government subsidizes Amtrak to keep the business going, though Chris is adamant that rumors of Amtrak folding are nonsense. "The stuff you read in the paper isn't correct," he insists. "They say that Amtrak is going to stop running. They can't! They never will, because of their contracts with the unions." The same unions Mike Farnsworth cursed as their demise? "Down in the northeast corner, if you stop running a train for two or three days, New York would turn into a parking lot."

Maybe…but probably not from only ceasing passenger service. The gas shortage of 1973 created a brief demand for rail travel, but the boom that sold out seventeen passenger cars in one day in Montpelier busted quickly. The gas price hike of 2005, as maligned as it was, barely affected the number of passengers leaving White River Junction.

But there are five lines through White River Junction again, Chris says, just the same as there were five during the glory days. "In 1848 you had the Vermont Central, Passumpsic Railroad, and the Northern Railroad of New Hampshire," he explains, fairly glowing with ninth inning hope. "When I came here in 1990, you had the Vermont Central, which was the Central Vermont at one time, then you had the B&M, then you had Amtrak. Now you have five different roads again, whereas one time you also had five different roads. It's a repeat of history."

He sees—if not exactly an 1850s-style boom—at least some growth in railroad traffic. "The future of the railroad in White River is going to grow!" he exclaims. Chris has no shortage of hope, and this morning, there's no shortage of silence along the line. "This winter, it went up maybe one or two percent, car-wise. The year before that, it went up five percent," growing more excited, "and the year before that it went up ten percent." But on the time line, those numbers are trending downwards: ten percent growth, five percent, to one percent. Still, his enthusiasm has me straining to hear a far off *chugga-chugga*.

I thank Chris for his time, earnestly promising to return soon so I can relive—in a small way—the glory days on the weekend excursion train. I walk north up the tracks, away from the station, following the course the Abigail Adams charted a century and a half before. The buildings along Railroad Row are now eateries, desk-job business offices, a Post Office and the Briggs Opera House. The Hotel Coolidge is still there across from the tracks, overlooking a grassy park, a parking lot, and the Vermont District Court. No trains blare their horns at me, and none come clacking past on the other rails. I bend down this afternoon, the station behind me like the last hundred fifty years, and touch a polished rail.

It's vibrating.

Top: The Cross-Abbott Building, probably the luckiest building in White River Junction, in its present form: Vermont Salvage.

Bottom: A projector for sale inside, where groceries once watired for their trains.

Treasure Hunting in
Civilization's Parts Department

Morning light draws yellow squares on a bare wooden floor. They are large squares, leaning slightly, longer than the huge doorways in the eastern wall of the Cross-Abbott warehouse. Crates are stacked high between the openings; brown steel bands hold bulging barrels in shape. The walls are unfinished, in places showing the backsides of the clapboard siding and the studs that shape the building. Every board is large, every beam is heavy, the construction meant to last through hard use and harder winters beyond the foreseeable future. It took teams of men days to hoist the beams in place, and would take a major catastrophe to disturb them—they barely quiver even as the ground shakes from the constant train traffic just yards away.

A man in brown wool pants and a linen shirt, fabric hat and black leather shoes, leans out from one of these doorways and cranes his neck around to look south down the railroad siding toward Springfield, Massachusetts. The 494, a giant steam locomotive, chugs slowly up the siding pulling three red boxcars through a switch and alongside the building. The boxcars block the sun, casting the loading dock in shadow as men emerge from the far corners of the warehouse to slide the boxcar doors open and unload towers of crates.

They set to work with the sort of fervor that wears

off by lunchtime, each man lifting or dragging as much as he can carry. Some take thin-paneled wooden crates, held together by wires, to the rear of the warehouse. Others load cloth sacks of potatoes and onions onto a wooden elevator platform. When the floor space is full they throw a lever on the electrical control box and the elevator lowers smoothly into the basement. The platform rides atop a massive piston that extends more than two stories below the basement floor. Though electricity is still novel for much of the village, here it runs a water pump that pressurizes a hydraulic tube. The piston extends under heavy water pressure as if growing from the ground itself to push the platform up from the basement to the main floor or beyond to the second floor. When the pressure is released, it descends along wooden tracks in the walls that keep the platform from swaying or binding, lowering until it reaches the basement where it sits now with a team of burly men dragging away large sacks of vegetables.

The basement walls are stone on the bottom and brick from waist height up to the ceiling. This part of New England is dangerously cold in the winter and rarely hot in the summer; insulated by the ground against these extremes, the cellar protects food from freezing or spoiling. Sacks of potatoes and onions, barrels of apples and other produce can wait awhile down here before riding off to market. Small windows with leaded glass panes let in some light, other light coming from the succession of bulbs that pulse and flicker with minor surges. Electricity has come to White River Junction, and so this morning have the trains with loads of passengers, mail, coal, fur, lumber, and produce.

Back on the main floor the men load boxcars with

groceries ordered by retailers. A shipment of wheat, corn, and barley from Massachusetts is forwarded north with a load of local produce from the Upper Connecticut Valley.

And so begins another day at the Cross-Abbott grocery wholesale business in their warehouse at the eastern terminus of Gates Street in White River Junction. While men in wool pants and white shirts scurry through the corridors between great stacks of crates and barrels, one man stands to the side, watching. He wears a business suit with dust around the ankles, fine black shoes with scuffs and cuts from crates he's moved. This man is Charles C. Abbott of Keene, New Hampshire, the co-owner of this company that bears his name.

Mr. Abbott stands regally, with the pride of great accomplishment. Turning around, he reads the cargo manifest while walking over the plank wood floor to his office near the front. He passes the elevator on his left, then the staircase to the second floor—more storage space—and pushes open the door to his office in the northwest corner. Charles Cross is inside scrutinizing an order for several hundred pounds of various produce needed in Montpelier the next afternoon, reconciling it with a train schedule. More than forty trains come through White River Junction each day. Most of them are freightliners, so scheduling one for the run north to the state capital should be simple. The men don't look at each other as Mr. Abbott lays the cargo manifest upon his partner's desk; they are so familiar by now that nothing needs to be said. The day is just getting started, another late autumn weekday in the Green Mountains. Mr. Abbott takes out his pocket watch, clicking open the brass case—nine-thirty.

My own watch reads nine-thirty just over a century later as I stand in that same office, watching for their ghosts. Gone is the old green-and-gold Cross-Abbott Co. Wholesale Grocers sign out front, replaced by one that reads Vermont Salvage. 114 years after its 1895 construction, this building has seen some of the most consistent and successful business in the town's history—despite the Great Depression's sledge-hammer blow, and even through the economically stagnant 1980s and 1990s. Its story is one of resounding success, a stark counterpoint to the town's dissolution in the mid twentieth century. Now the successful Vermont Salvage is a crypt for the bones of older, failed buildings—doors salvaged from schools, cabinets from homes, stained glass windows taken from churches just ahead of the wrecking ball... When old buildings die, the choice bits are interred in salvage shops like this.

Ed Mosher stares up at me from his desk in the front office, a thin curl of cigarette smoke dancing in the air between us. "It's a great old building, I tell ya," he says, stabbing the air with the glowing ash to emphasize his point. Ed is the father in law of Jesse LaBombard—the company's owner, a middle aged man sitting across the office in front of a computer—and a good source of information on what's happened here in the last two decades, but not before. "Nineteen years ago I turned sixty five," he says, "and I moved up from Massachusetts, that's how I remember. My daughter married the guy who owns the place." That same year he moved north "to be with her," he said. Ed doesn't know much about what happened here before Vermont Salvage moved into the 30,000 square foot warehouse in 1990, so he points out the door and says "there's a sign on the front that tells you everything about it."

"Everything about it" comes in three short paragraphs and a black and white photo familiar from page 121 in John St. Croix's <u>Historical Highlights of the Town of Hartford Vermont</u>. The local historical society posted that sign in honor of the building's place on the National Register of Historic Buildings, but it only satisfies casual curiosity. You can learn from it how the Cross-Abbott Company "dealt exclusively in groceries, was one of the village's thirteen thriving wholesale businesses in 1903," and moved on to bigger facilities in 1957, but not much more. It stops far short of saying "everything" about a building with such a unique place in the town's history.

I came to poke around the dusty warehouse and find the edges of just that place in the sands of time, and perhaps to find treasure buried here between a deteriorating, vacant house and rusty railroad tracks on the decrepit east end of Gates Street.

* * * * *

"Yup, there's some treasure back there," Ed says after a minute of chewing on his words and the butt of his cigarette. "I think the most interesting was probably a couple English telephone booths we had from England. These were straight from England, big bucks, but by God we sold 'em," he says with the satisfaction of a man who just sold an icebox to an Eskimo. "Like I say, you never know what the hell's coming through here."

Indeed, the unpredictable variety of salvage coming through the front loading door keeps things mighty interesting. Stephen Gordon of the local newspaper, the Valley News, paid them a visit in the 1990s. "Walk into Vermont Salvage Exchange on Railroad Row," he wrote, "and you get the feeling you're in Civilization's parts department." Their inventory consists of doors, bathroom fixtures, altars, chairs, bottles, mantles, light fixtures...anything left behind for the wrecking crew that Jesse thinks has resale value. This includes, in the front display window, two antique dentist chairs complete with instrument trays, several tools, and spit sinks—straight out of the 1940s. One man's junk is Vermont Salvage's special of the month.

To paraphrase Frank Miller's classic line, "Walk down the right back alley in Vermont Salvage and you can find anything." The possibilities, like the diversity of wares, are so vast and changing as to feel limitless. But is there actual treasure in Civilization's parts department? And is this National Register landmark a true historical treasure, or just another old building? To find out, I thank Ed for his time and mosey into the dark warehouse.

There are few windows here, so most of the light comes from bare bulbs strung overhead. Floodlights clamped to the rafters hang over rows of doors, and a fluorescent light tube glows on a wooden mantelpiece. The wooden floor is laid so the planks reach deeper into the warehouse, drawing my gaze along a row of hanging bulbs towards the very soul of the building. There is a wide walkway through the middle of the warehouse, so you can move large items in and out easily, with little alleys leading off between arrangements of concrete figures, rows of doors, bathtubs, cabinets...

They might not have truly everything, but they do

have the kitchen sink—several dozen different sinks, actually. And there are dozens of doors, hundreds of doors, maybe thousands of doors, stacked in rows in this warehouse. What did they open into? There is something strange about seeing doors that don't open into anything, whole stacks of doors that open into nothing but the next door in line.

The loading doors along the eastern wall are fixed in place, as they are more useful as walls than passageways now that the railroad siding has been torn up. Unlike its predecessors, Vermont Salvage doesn't make use of the railroads, so convenient access to boxcars is unnecessary; they no longer even have rails upon which to sidle alongside the building. The doors fade into the background—just more edges and incongruous contours in a rich visual field.

There could be treasure just about anywhere. There are mounds of junk topped with treasure, mounds of junk burying treasure, mounds of junk with no treasure anywhere near them and then one treasure by itself in a corner. There is a display case near one door that is full of hinges and faceplates from skeleton key locks. A lot of these hinges still have their original lead-based paint, which has cracked and flaked over time and looks like reptilian scales on the brass. There are a few with molded designs—they look Victorian but aren't. You can refinish a bathroom in classic style with a porcelain doorknob for $25 or a glass knob for $15. These are the hand-selected parts; the rest are in bins nearby.

Beyond the case is a stained glass window depicting St. Vincent DePaul showing a crucifix to a child. The pane is six feet tall and hangs in front of a dusty window so that the saint glows between dark wooden walls.

Overhead is the lower terminus of a wooden chute where Cross-Abbott workers could slide crates from the second floor right down to the loading area. You have to look for the chute, but it is there, as sure as the history of this building is accessible if you look closely enough. Every scratch in the floor holds a story like the grooves on a record—the secret is making history sing to you.

Before I root through the buckets of old skeleton keys or bins of mismatched doorknobs, I consider the construction of the wall near the stained glass window. It is built with large timbers running from the floor to the ceiling every foot or so, to which are attached the horizontal six inch wide by two inch thick boards that comprise the outer wall. There is no particle board, no plywood, no vinyl siding on the outside or plastic lining inside. This building was built to last two or three hundred years, if not more. The bare wood swells and shrinks with the humidity. The clapboard siding faces the elements with disregard for the weather. Everything speaks of solid craftsmanship—an investment in the future. White River Junction was thirty years into its growth spurt by 1895, and still then three decades shy of the town's Great Depression bust. Cross and Abbott had every reason to believe that they needed a building that could outlast them, their children, and their children's children...which is exactly what they built.

Charles Abbott started in the grocery business in Keene, New Hampshire, and brought this experience to his association with Charles Cross. After successfully running a fuel oil distribution business together, they leased a fifty foot by one hundred foot parcel of land from the Central Vermont Railroad. That land became the site of the Cross-Abbott Co. wholesale grocery business, and the building here described.

They operated the grocery business out of the small office on the main floor of this building along the railroad tracks for the rest of their lives. The business remained here even after its founders were long past, the trains arriving to load and unload all manner of groceries for distribution north into the Green Mountains or for sale in big cities far to the south.

Then fires destroyed the train depot thirty yards away, the prominent Junction House Hotel less than one hundred yards away, Isaac Gates' chair factory, and the White River Paper Company—twice each, actually. Each of those landmarks burned once before the Cross-Abbott Co., and once each afterwards. Other businesses and homes also burned, and the railroad was no stranger to fiery disasters involving their wooden bridges. With so much fire reshaping downtown White River Junction, given that the wooden warehouse was highly flammable, and considering its proximity to so many of those conflagrations, it is miraculous that Cross and Abbott never suffered such a loss. Their fortune held, even as the village around them was buffeted by disasters financial and natural.

The city hosted fairs from 1890 until 1900, when they were discontinued due to lack of solvency. The State Fair came to town in 1907, and the city tried to make a go of hosting fairs again until poor attendance—in large part due to poor weather—forced them to abandon the idea in 1928. The White River rerouted itself down Main Street in West Hartford Village during the Flood of 1927, washing away buildings and flooding cellars, but again, Cross-Abbott weathered the calamity. The Great Depression followed soon after the last fair, ravaging businesses and private fortunes and resulting in the turnover of companies like the Smith & Son-come-Vermont Baking Co. and the Junction House-come-Hotel Coolidge. While the thirteen wholesale businesses that comprised Railroad Row struggled to stay solvent through the hard times, Cross-Abbott stands out as one of the businesses that thrived in spite of recession.

On September 28, 1938, the lingering Great Depression was made even worse by the hurricane that hit New England...and battered White River Junction. Trees were uprooted and windows smashed in the freak storm; power lines were downed and started small fires and several doors on the Hotel Coolidge were broken, but the worst damage the Cross-Abbott building sustained was a blown-over chimney.

The town did not fully recover from the Great Depression, even in the prosperous times after World War II. But Cross-Abbott maintained their business, operating through everything. When the Red & White Corporation showed interest in acquiring the wholesaler in 1948, the two companies merged. They adapted their business model to make use of delivery vehicles, which could ferry goods from train depots to wherever stores happened to be. The business grew such that they built a new facility across the White River in downtown Hartford. Finished in 1957, the warehouse featured a 70,000 cubic foot freezer locker. Their staff swelled to more than three hundred employees. With no more need for the original Gates Street warehouse, they sold the facility to the White River Paper Company.

The new occupant was no young upstart, either—founded in 1881 by Alma C. Farman, George W. Smith, and Samuel L. Farman, White River Paper Company had operated continuously from various sites around town.

They added a concrete extension to the building that is easily discerned from the inside by the change in floor from worn planks to gray concrete. They made minimum alterations to the building itself, keeping the rear wall intact and using an existing loading door to connect the two interiors. Sometime in the middle of the century a covered loading dock was added to the front of the building, partially obscuring the old façade. A storefront display area, where the dentist chairs sit now, was added as well. Their careful maintenance of the building and the preservation of the Italianate Revival architecture suggests they respected history. They even kept the quoins on the corners that were used so often in late 1800s boom-era construction around White River Junction. Though the sign above the entryway changed names and an extension grew from the rear of the building, the heart of the structure remained the same… and its luck held.

* * * * *

I want to see the difference between old and new, to see if I can feel it, so I keep my eyes on the exposed beams overhead and marvel at the dark timbers until my footsteps turn from wooden clops into dull slaps on cold concrete. Overhead is the reinforced frame leading out of the old building and into the new. The southern wall of the old structure, now an interior wall, is the same clapboard that once kept nor'easter winds and snow at bay. The walls here are made of gray cinder blocks, the ceiling supported by bright red I-beams and round steel posts. Even though the full length of this connected warehouse is unheated, this chamber feels colder than the one before.

Pallets of paper, books, postcards, all sorts of printed goods and raw materials, filled this room. Now it's filled with cabinets salvaged from schools and institutions, great stacks of identical brown cupboards, a pile of oak boards with tongue-and-groove-cut edges, and a stack of rectangular pressed-tin ceiling panels. The salvage here is not as old as that in the previous chamber, nor as interesting as the history of the Paper Company that built this room.

They prospered under several presidents while in the Cross-Abbott building. The fires that plagued their early days in the Smith Block and at the train depot—where on January 2nd, 1888, they suffered a $4,500 loss to fire in a time when a good day's wage was $0.76—did not trouble them here. As train traffic dropped off and the mainstay businesses of Railroad Row slowly folded or moved elsewhere, the Paper Company made wise business moves and stayed ahead of the downturns.

In 1973 Ed Nichols became president of the company and diversified their product offerings to include office supplies. The natural pairing of one office mainstay—paper—with others helped keep the company lucrative.

Across town in George W. Smith's old bakery, the Ward Baking Company was struggling to stay solvent. In 1974 they succumbed to the rampant fiscal rot, and over the next two decades their building was cursed with one failed business after another. Other buildings along Railroad Row fell to similar fates, or outright abandonment. Hippies selling all manner of salvage and miscellany inhabited four such buildings just yards

52

north of White River Station—their buildings were leaky, in disrepair, and on their way out. That the White River Paper Company flourished in such a place and time is an outright miracle.

But flourish they did, outgrowing even their expanded facilities. In 1986 Peter Lyford and his sons bought controlling shares of the company's stock and custom-built a new facility just a few miles away on Route 14 in Hartford. They prepared to vacate the Gates Street location while across the tracks a strange turn of events threatened to leave Jesse LaBombard with four buildings worth of salvage and nowhere to go with it.

Ed's stories from this morning come to mind, picking up the history within that nineteen year window he knows firsthand. The hippies set up their business in the old Twin State Fruit Co. facility and surrounding buildings. Members gradually left the commune, leaving control to David Furr. He sold the business to Jesse LaBombard in the 1980s. Business continued until the State of Vermont eyed the property for the site of a new courthouse. It was to be an investment in the city, a civic project that would bring work to the area and traffic through the decaying downtown, and keep White River Junction on the minds of legislators with public money to spend.

"They kicked us the hell out," Ed grumbled to me this morning. Jesse's voice comes to mind as well, adding how "they used eminent domain. They threw us out to build the courthouse." With nowhere to go, they looked all over New Hampshire and Vermont before finally settling on the Cross-Abbott building just a block away. "We basically just moved in," Jesse said. "We had to make racks for the doors, but, it was a big, empty

building, and it fit our needs. We need a lot of space."
They purchased the facility and moved their inventory
just ahead of the bulldozers. The Cross-Abbott building
had barely been vacated when the first salvage crossed
through the loading door. Vermont Salvage is only the
third business to occupy the building in 114 years of
near-continuous occupancy.

Even the Cross-Abbott Co. did not go out of
business like virtually all of the 1800s-era companies in
White River Junction. They lost their identity through
corporate mergers, but never officially failed. The
White River Paper Company is still in strong operation
in their new facility on Route 14, and Vermont Salvage
just celebrated their nineteenth year at the end of
Gates Street. The building has never burned. By such
accounts, it is possibly the luckiest building in White
River Junction.

Which brings us back to this chilly November
morning standing just inside the concrete extension at
the rear of the building, where the unheated air is not
quite cold enough to freeze my breath. The identical
cupboards stacked to my left were cut by machine,
not fashioned by hand, and lack that sense of character
usually found in the furniture at salvage shops. The goods
in this room, save the tin ceiling segments, are hardly
older than me. They lack character from individuality or
age; bottle up this room like wine, let the times change
with the calendars, and perhaps in thirty years these
goods will be more interesting. I walk farther down the
central corridor, trying to imagine what it looked like as
a warehouse for the paper company; conjuring images
of identical cardboard boxes is even less appealing than
looking at the cupboards.

54

But then things change, and the lighter institutional wood takes a turn for darker colors, pine giving way to teak, and I find myself in a very different section of the store indeed: this is called East India Salvage, a few thousand square feet of floor space given over to Charlie Miller's enterprise. A friend of Ed and Jesse, Charlie travels to India and other exotic locales in search of anything he can ship back for resale in the United States. That his name is the same as both of the original owners is a coincidence I can't overlook.

His contribution is this dense jumble of teak armoires and handsome bookcases. There are cabinets and dressers, a few paintings of Hindu gods, and even bamboo wind chimes of unknown origin—marked down half price to only nine dollars. There are British colonial doors with ornate carvings and strong iron bars over their windows. The furniture here is heavy, the kind that heartily endured years of use and then a trans-pacific voyage, trans-continental shipment, and storage in an obscure, unheated building in Vermont. The scars on their façades and corners are noble, the kinds that suggest authenticity, durability, character—attributes not found in modern particleboard-and-veneer furniture.

Most notable among the offerings is a painting called "The Passover Instituted," by Thomas Nelson and Sons, which depicts a scene from Exodus XII, but set in India: a Hebrew man paints lamb's blood over his doorway for Passover, while an Indian Guru and his entourage look on admiringly. This image of two cultures communing under a splotch of lamb's blood on a door frame is no less jarring than finding Indian furniture in Vermont—which is to say that both are shocking, but together make a strange kind of sense.

The essence of the building is not really in this concrete room, and while the foreign salvage is interesting, White River Junction's history is not in dressers from India; I walk quickly towards the front again, towards the historic main building full of strange delights.

Like the grocery business, Vermont Salvage has a claim to Massachusetts. Charles Cross hailed from Fitchburg, Massachusetts, where he lived and worked before moving to White River Junction. Charles Abbott owned Abbott Grocery in Athol, Massachusetts. When the town's newspaper, the *Landmark*, announced that a new business was coming to Railroad Row on November 24, 1893, they wrote that "a number of Massachusetts gentlemen...will erect a large building in which to carry on a wholesale grocery business." They maintained ties with Massachusetts throughout their lives. Now Vermont Salvage employs Ed, a Massachusetts man, and gets most of its inventory from renovations there as well. Surprisingly, Vermont Salvage has very little salvage from White River Junction...or even Vermont.

"A lot of it comes out of Massachusetts," Ed told me earlier today. "We work hand in glove with quite a few demolition companies. The Catholic churches are starting to call us now when they're closing down a church. That's good stuff." But despite renovations to the firehouse on Bridge Street, the Tip Top Building on North Main Street, and other projects in the area, not many bits of local history are offered for sale here. "We deal a lot in architectural antique salvage," he had said, "and there's just not that much around White River." He seemed surprised when I mentioned a 1920s-era movie projector that I noticed on a previous trip through

56

the warehouse. "I didn't know there was even one out there."

I'm standing in front of it now, a machine slightly taller than me if you count the two and a half foot tall stovepipe vent coming out of the light chamber. It used some of the earliest electric bulbs, the kind that put out as much heat as light. Turn it on, rotate the lens cover out of the way, and projectionists could bring Douglas Fairbanks to life on the silent silver screen. Projectors much like this one brought to life the heroes of my grandfather's age, like Tom Mix, and stars of my father's childhood, like John Wayne. Here it stands: a piece of history familiar across the ages, several hundred pounds of aluminum and steel, something Ed forgot they have.

Jesse remembered it, though, and told me it came from Massachusetts. "I found it in some kind of state hospital. They had a little room upstairs. I had to drag it out." I asked how much he wanted for it, and he rolled his eyes a moment before saying "Oh, about fifteen hundred."

I peruse the aisles and corners again, looking over the dusty mantelpieces and sinks, a five-foot-long steel bathtub, and of course, the rows of doors that seem to lengthen when you're not looking. I pass the elevator with its steel chains coated in dusty grease. They attach to counterweights in the walls that weigh around forty-five percent of the maximum loaded elevator weight, making the job easier for the pneumatic ram that pushes it up and down. It still works, over one hundred years later—another part of the building designed for the ages. Jesse regularly uses it to move salvage between floors.

There is a white arrow painted on the planks that leads me along a stack of doors to one white door that is actually—surprisingly—attached to a wall. It stands open, inviting me to walk down into the basement. The smell of earth and age boil up the wooden stairwell like steam.

Down here are windows. As there are interminable rows of doors upstairs, here are endless rows of windows: newer windows, older windows, very, very old windows, windows painted white, windows varnished brown, windows with chipped glass, windows with broken glass, windows until I'm sick of the very word. This basement is in the older part of the building, and in the older part of the building only: no extension was dug for the expansion, though there is a second original room towards the rear of the building.

The second room has shutters: green shutters, orange shutters, yellow and brown, black, blue, colors faded and chipped, colors solid and bold. Several small windows in the foundation let in a minimum of morning sunlight. Overhead are solid wooden beams and a sprinkler system added sometime in the early 1900s to defend against the fires that plagued White River Junction's other landmarks. Despite more than one hundred years of must, there is little wrong with the basement—no termites, no signs of rats or even mice...Charles Abbott could be proud of his building.

I walk back upstairs, round the corner at the end of the stack of doors, and walk towards the front of the warehouse. There is a stairwell to the second story, but I visited there earlier and found little of interest— as fascinating as a large, cluttered warehouse can be, the appeal gets stretched thin through a tour of three similar floors. The salvage up there was either boxed in white cardboard labeled "stovepipe" or simply more of the same fixtures and dusty clutter as below, and in any event, not terribly interesting.

Walking towards the front of the warehouse now, I peer inside the office. Ed is gone, so I wave to Jesse and he gives me a smile. In the cavernous room behind me are stacks and piles and pieces of history—pieces of Massachusetts' history, mainly. But this warehouse storing them is distinctly part of White River Junction. There is treasure inside after all, but not the kind you hope to find in the bottom of a salvage bin. This vestige of White River Junction's Great American Dream was not ravaged by the Great Depression, the transportation revolution, fire, natural disaster, or time. It is living history that offers you a ride on the same elevator that generations of foremen rode before you. It has a certain magic, a certain feel, and its current inventory changes often enough to give you reason to keep coming back to the luckiest building in White River Junction.

Hotel Coolidge—Though it burned down several times, the Hotel Coolidge arose from the ashes each time as a symbol of the town's hope and prospects.

Caught Between Eras
Discovering the Hotel Coolidge

Any good railroad town needs a grand hotel, somewhere near the depot with enough rooms for everyone when the trains pull in for the night. White River Junction's railroad hotel was the Junction House, right across the tracks from the station. In operation since the mid nineteenth century, it greeted a President, burned down twice, was sold many times, and still rents rooms. Early light makes the red bricks glow this morning on the Hotel Coolidge, the modern incarnation of Nathanial Wheeler's original hotel here on South Main Street; today I hope to find a bit of rail-era majesty inside this landmark.

Two square, brick towers rise above the third story; one is the proprietor's apartment, and the other is in semi-permanent renovation limbo. The hotel is a horseshoe, with two wings leading west around a tiny parking lot. The guest rooms are on the second and third floors; on the street level around the lobby are various stores and boutiques; Coolidge Cards is their official gift shop. Autumn wind swirls leaves under the blue and white awning over the entrance, tugging at the ruffles and slipping inside as I open the glass front doors.

I step inside under the stern gaze of John Coolidge, the hotel's namesake, staring down at me from an oil painting opposite the entrance. To the right is Inky's

Café, a self-service café where you may sometimes find a carafe of coffee or pitcher of water; there are several tables and booths, a piano and a fireplace. The lobby is on my left, with three couches and several chairs, a desk, another piano, and a fireplace—the main floor is not short on fireplaces, nor on pianos, sporting three of each between the various rooms. Guests wander past me to the front desk, an office built out of a corner between the Zollikofer Gallery and a bathroom.

Most of the guests today, Wednesday, are here with an Elderhostel group. While the Hotel Coolidge has been a White River Junction landmark for 156 years, several of the Hostel folks are older than the present building—this is possible because of how beautifully the Hotel Coolidge's story reflects the fears for—and fates of—so many buildings a century ago. But more of the hostellers now…

They've driven across New England, one gentleman from as far as California, to tour and study small town history. They came to learn about the hotel, White River Junction, the New England railroad, and how the fates of each were so entwined.

I walk past the desk, smile at the receptionist, and down the short hallway towards the Vermont Room. The hallway walls comprise the Zollikofer Gallery, and today, show large prints made by a local newspaper photographer. In one photo a bee crawls across a pink flower; another features a beautiful countryside bereft any buildings. These works are all for sale, and occasionally a piece will sell. The adhoc gallery is dedicated to August L. Zollikofer, the Italian-American who owned the hotel "at two different times from 1946 until 1970," a brochure explains. New displays grace the old walls six times a year, offering a special treat to regular lodgers...but the most impressive art in the building is the Vermont Room mural at the end of the hall, where a history class will begin momentarily.

This dining room hosts wedding receptions, college formals, political speeches (Republican heavyweights Bob Dole, Jack Kemp, and others visited the Hotel Coolidge in '88 to stump for George Bush Sr.), and many other gatherings. Dartmouth College graduate and artist Peter Gish negotiated with Zollikofer in 1950 for a creative exchange: room and board at the hotel for Gish painting a mural in the Vermont room. He used oil paint to record a history of Vermont in a panorama that commands three walls. Beginning with a tableau of Indians and settlers, it honors the Revolutionary War, the opening of the West, the twentieth century's armed conflicts, and Vermonters' indomitable spirits. The scenes flow easily from one to another, each captured in dark colors further shadowed by years of soot from the fireplace. They burn gas in that fireplace now, but time's unkind effects are as central to the ambiance as the paintings and furniture.

The room fills with Elderhostel students, and I shake hands with David Briggs, the hotel's current proprietor and a native White River Junction man with keen interest in history and the restoration of classic buildings. He welcomes me in that friendly-while-guarded, hospitable but don't get too close Vermont way. The story at hand, of the Hotel Coolidge and White River Junction, is dear to him; he carefully selects his words during the presentation and corrects his audience when they proffer inaccurate conclusions. With the gas fire burning low this morning he flips on an overhead projector and introduces himself to the group.

Two hours later I have fourteen pages of notes, but more importantly, I have a better understanding of this landmark hotel and where it fits in local history. David answers my last few questions as the students shuffle through a door to the elegant Junction Room for lunch at fancy tables below glass chandeliers. The class is over, but my journey through the hotel's history is just getting interesting.

* * * * *

Moments ago the receptionist handed me two keys, looking at me with outright suspicion. On prior visits I only poked around the main floor, gazing in awe at the comic book covers hanging in Inky's Café or wandering reverently through the Zollikofer Gallery. But then I wanted access to the rooms, and only when I assured her of Mr. Briggs's consent did she cautiously give me two keys. I bounded up the stairs from the lobby to what they call the "first floor," a level above the street and a story above the town.

I face room 105, the first door on the left. On a table in the hallway sits a reddish-brown, bulbous, hideous lamp from the 60s under a mirror where I looked at myself looking back through time. The door opens with a metal key—not the modern electric key card system, but the kind with which you open a door in your home. Pushing it open I'm greeted with the strangely familiar smell of a comfortable room—not the antiseptic air in chain hotels, but the essence of grandma's living room. It smells faintly of so many people, though distinctly of no one—comforting redolence.

The history of this room is the history of those who made White River Junction: railroad workers and business travelers who spent nights at the Hotel Coolidge; moguls and minions and politicos and newlyweds. Each left a smell, a scratch, a mark, part of the ambience and part of themselves, like fingerprints. There's a sturdy, dark wooden desk under the framed stencil of a garden, pen scratches worn into the grain.

Windows on each side of the desk face the old Post Office and its white granite corner blocks. Framed by the walls, the windows overlook old brick buildings in the historic downtown, the top of an old fashioned lamppost across the street, the green clapboard façade on an old general store, and a timeless blue sky. High brick archways frame windows in a corner building, with brick crosses mortared in place between the second floor and the roof.

The walls in this room are light white, one papered with an ascending floral design of light pink and blue flowers. Runners from this vertical garden grow laterally along a paper border that circles the room, slipping below each of two P.J. Redoute prints—flowers, his specialty. A framed mirror with heavy, dark wood hangs in the center of that wall, just beyond a door that opens to the right. Though mid fall, with chilly winds blowing outside, the room is warm; in the winter it will be heated by the single radiator in the far left corner that stands near an open door into the bathroom.

The bed commands the floor; a white linen top sheet decorated with rich patterns covers a firm mattress. These are the sheets you find in homes, the sheets grandmothers and great aunts washed in the first electric washing machines brought into White River Junction a half century ago. They are comforting, a break in the routine of cloned Holiday Inn sterility—a touch as personal as it is historic. There is a headboard, stained to match the other furniture in the room, which fits just a quarter inch from being flush with the wall. Either it is off, or the wall is off, a tiny imperfection that proves each was made by hand in some bygone era by real people building furniture and rooms for other real people. I expect to see the craftsman's fingerprints enshrined in the varnish, but find none.

There beside the bed is a nightstand with a brass lamp and a Gideon Bible in the drawer. The only furniture out of place among the dark-stained wood is a pink, red, salmon, and blue striped easy chair—overstuffed—facing the windows. It looks strange but feels right. Everything about this room suggests a time before standardization, before chain-store familiarity and furniture ordered by the thousand. You know what to expect from a Holiday Inn; you can't anticipate the look or feel inside the Hotel Coolidge, even from room to room.

That leaves plenty of room for surprises.

I am standing pretty far back in the past, save two anachronisms: the cable-access television and a white plastic telephone. The door could be a portal to another time, a room trapped in the past, save these conveniences. The television sits upon a low dresser, facing the bed; framed in black plastic, the dull reflection of the room on its blank screen is far less interesting than the panorama framed in the window.

Careful not to disturb the chambermaid's work, I turn left towards a door near the radiator; it leads into a spacious, white-tiled bathroom. The corner is beveled, adding a narrow fifth wall to the room. Local historian David Ford told me that the hotel was built upon an irregularly shaped lot, and perhaps this tiny section is one of the concessions made to accommodate the design; or it could conceal pipes and ductwork—even boring possibilities must be considered.

Walking back into the bedroom, I walk past the windows and spare a glance at the street below. The sight of modern sedans and sport utility vehicles between this room and the spectacular granite faux columns on the old Post Office is a bit jarring. There is another door, opposite the foot of the bed, standing open just an inch as if to invite me to pull it open. Inside is a long, thin closet with five tarnished brass coat hooks, a shelf on the right, and a sprinkler overhead. Everywhere in this hotel, in these rooms and hallways—apparently in the closets as well—there are sprinklers.

They were installed throughout the building in the 1930s at the behest of then-owner Col. Nathanial Wheeler to thwart the series of fires which destroyed first one, then two previous incarnations of the hotel. Fire consumed the railroad station across the tracks on a number of occasions, and ravaged homes and businesses throughout the village; no wonder he embraced the "new" technology. There are two rows of sprinklers running through this room, one of which enters the bathroom while the other terminates here in the closet.

I close the door, and daydream a bit—what could have been here, in this space, in the original hotel? With being rebuilt and remodeled so often, the times changing to where we expect, now, a full private bathroom in every room, this one suite could have been two or three; as I walk back to the overstuffed chair, am I walking through the ghosts of walls burned twice?

Above street level with its contemporary cars and signs for modern businesses, the stone walls and arches along the far side of South Main Street are the same now as ever; this view is perhaps the least-changed aspect of this space over the last hundred years. Even the aqua-green trim on a building across the way seems to fit, drawn into this room by and matched perfectly to the elbow covers on the overstuffed chair. Close your eyes and imagine yourself in the Junction House in 1894; open them in this room, and there's little to suggest you're only pretending. The synergy of interior and exterior in this mostly timeless room has a soothing effect, slowing life to three miles an hour—walking speed in a village built on a pedestrian scale.

* * * * *

They call this second story the "first floor," and it bears room numbers in the 100s. With no windows on the corridor and only soft lighting, mainly from lamps over flower arrangements on decorative tables, you get a powerful sense of walking through the very bowels of the hotel. The colors and darkness—even at noon—keep conversations quiet as middle-aged and elderly patrons wander the halls; the gloom is a striking counterpoint that makes the airy, white-walled rooms seem all the brighter.

Bearing right, towards a distant staircase and the rest of the Gates-Briggs Block of contiguous buildings, I find an alcove with three windows, two couches, and a coffee table strewn with decade-old magazines. Recent history interposes between that of the old hotel and the present afternoon here as I find the August 1993 issue of Good Housekeeping peeking out from below the July 1994 issue of the same. I place them side by side, the one on the left featuring Princess Diana—alive and well for the photo shoot in 1993, she died August 31st, 1997. The issue beside it features Jacqueline Kennedy Onassis. Jackie died May 19, 1994, before the July issue hit stands but after the deadline for the article on page 108 that refers to her in the living.

These cover girls are probably not the only ghosts in the Hotel Coolidge, so I sit here quietly and hope that one will waft by—perhaps carrying a candle to light their way, or reading a long forgotten copy of the *Landmark*. That paper would be a ghost here, too—it dissolved in 1952 after being bought out by the Valley News; a copy of that periodical occupies a far corner of this coffee table. These are all parts of the hotel's patchwork—hallways that bend and bulge with gently sloping floors, narrow fifth-walls in trapezoidal bathrooms, dead celebrities still alive on magazine covers from a decade ago…it's easy to lose yourself in the Hotel Coolidge.

The longer I sit, waiting for history to engage me, the more I engage this building: the floor is not brown and black, but dark green, pink, and black, in swirling patterns like palm fronds in a hurricane. Darkness tinges the pink and green to shades of brown, and suggests—falsely, as living history is prone to do—that they match the dark-stained furniture in the hallway. The banister post at the foot of the stairs leans almost twenty degrees north, the floor sloping two gradual inches downward as the hallway bends around and below the staircase. Overhead, a crossbeam in the ceiling bends in the middle, perhaps where it needed to lower slightly to meet another beam. Trim running away along the ceiling curves like an old man's back. Square corners join curved trim, and straight trim meets in imperfect corners—few details are entirely what they seem at first, from colors to lines and the sense of history not as old as it would like to suggest. The couch beside me was ripped long ago by a cane, or a broken button, or... There in two places on the center cushion are hand-stitched seams, one closing an L-shaped wound with thread that matches the cushion.

History flows inexorably, as quickly towards the future as away from the past, like the Connecticut River just two blocks east—but history flows through space, changing the carpet, warping old boards, leaving upon everything that dust which rises in gray clouds when you slap the couch cushions. History is the men who worked on flatboats before the trains, the tough men who stood for hours on barges and guided them with poles and paddles—it forges on with unfaltering steps, and like those flatboat river men in the old saloons, fills the gaps in its stories with lurid inventions. This building looks historic, feels historic, and in many ways, truly is historic—older than most of the working men in White River Junction today. But it was born only eighty years ago, making it younger than some of its lodgers.

Its predecessor burned in 1925; later that year, the building I'm sitting in was built to mostly the same specifications. The towers I'm familiar with, rising two stories each from atop the third story roof, used to be topped with steeples—and used to have a fourth floor between them. The clocks on the southern tower froze years ago, and the round sign on the old northern tower was not duplicated in this reconstruction. "It was rebuilt in a hurry with a wood frame," David Briggs explained in his presentation. "It was reopened in such a hurry that they didn't even finish the top floor."

The four story structure this building replaced was, itself, a replacement; the strange saga of the Hotel Coolidge begins in Enfield, New Hampshire, some thirteen miles away, in the mid 1800s. Enfield supported a hotel at the time, the Grafton House, which attracted the eye of Colonel Samuel Nutt.

Col Nutt was a riverboat captain, Civil War veteran, White River Junction's first Postmaster, and a local man of color and means. Estimating that White River Junction's railroad traffic and thriving downtown could support a hotel, he purchased the Grafton House in Enfield and had it dismantled and moved in pieces across the river to a site across the tracks from the train station. Its first customers in White River Junction were railroad workers, salesmen, and other visitors drawn to the boomtown.

As passenger service picked up, the clientele included foreign and domestic immigrants seeking new jobs at the mills and factories along the Ottauquechee, White, and Connecticut rivers, as well as statesmen and dignitaries. When the trains stopped for the evening at White River Station, passengers strolled the walkway between the tracks and Colonel Samuel Nutt's Junction House hotel.

The hotel overlooks the railroad yard, with the buildings of Railroad Row standing in the wings along North Main Street. Lodgers looked out over warehouses and workshops, livestock trading stations, and a wholesale grocer—Cross-Abbott. Like the hotel, these buildings were made of rugged wooden trusses and brick, multistory structures with solid roofs and walls built thick against the winter cold. Also like the original hotel, they had a quiet dignity and strength for the ages—a sign of faith in their town's prosperity and future. Brick archways over windows, commemorative corner stones, ornamental iron...the flourishes on the downtown buildings were tasteful and reflected the industrial work ethic that built the town. It was an age of businesses passed down through families, and structures built to last indefinitely...with the expectation that they would.

Seen from my modern age of job-hopping, disposable products, and house-flipping, the idea of building something to outlast my interest in it, and even my life—by decades—is as refreshing as it is novel. Yet that was the way late nineteenth century investors and businessmen, architects and masons saw their world— less in terms of dalliance, more in terms of legacy.

A few corners were cut, though; most obviously, in developing the land between the station and the hotel.

After hauling in enough sand to solidify the swampland to build the station, no one bothered to fill in the natural depression between the station and the Junction House. A walkway connected the station with the downtown area, and the depression below became a depository for all sorts of refuse. Discarded cans from the Twin State Fruit Corporation sank into mounds of coal ash; trash attracts more of itself with near-magnetic strength, and soon the walkway spanned not just a depression, but an open garbage pit. On July 18, 1890, the *Landmark* printed an editorial about the unsightly refuse.

I stand up from the couch and turn to the windows, looking over South Main Street to the tracks, over a parking lot where that scene was set in 1890. Lifting my copy of John St. Croix's book <u>Historical Highlights of the Town of Hartford, Vermont</u>, I read an excerpt from that historic article on the trash pit:

> If any person has old garbage that is an eyesore about their premises, the ground between the depot and the Landmark block will be found a convenient place of deposit. The pile already on the grounds is large but we presume the railroad folks will furnish more ground when needed. It isn't every village that offers such an attraction to the traveling public. How refreshing and restful it must be to the weary traveler who has been whirled along through green woods and fields, to let his eyes rest upon a pile of elegant red and yellow labeled fruit cans in a beautiful setting of coal ashes and broken bottles.

The town grew weary of giving this first impression to railway travelers, so the Loyal Club suggested they fill the depression and transform the space into an inviting park, construction of which was completed in 1901. With these improvements to the right-of-way and, by then, dozens of new churches and buildings, White River Junction was heading for its high water mark.

Leaving the windows behind, I walk past the stairwell, down the slight bend in the floor, and along a west-leading wing past the Coolidge Room. That name, the surname of Colonel John Coolidge and his famous son, thirtieth US President Calvin Coolidge, is omnipresent inside the hotel. Personal friends with Col.

Nathan Wheeler, Col. Coolidge was a frequent guest on his trips through White River Junction. When the President stayed at the Hotel in the 1920s, he chose this first floor room, Parlor A, out of a superstition about staying in numbered rooms.

The Elderhostel students began their tour today at President Coolidge's birthplace in Plymouth Notch, and will end it with a stop past Parlor A. In the second grade I prepared a report on his life and presidency, focusing on how he signed a bill in 1924 that made the American Indians official US citizens. Walking past a room where he once stayed, in a hotel that bears his family name, I feel a vast, powerful...nothing.

At least, nothing beyond the creative energy from these—unique—surroundings. I walk past David Briggs' office on the left side of this second story hallway, and stop just short of an anachronistic Coca~Cola machine. Here in this historic space, in a 1920s state of mind, the Coke machine seems quite out of place. But in a hotel with bathroom tile from the 1970s, furniture from the 1950s, architecture from the 1920s, and wireless internet access, why should there not be an electric Coke machine in the hallway?

There's a staircase here leading up to the third story, the top level of the hotel proper, which they call the "second floor." The rooms are numbered in the 200s, and I have a key to room 205. The two towers, one on the north end and one on the south, rise two stories beyond the roof; this "second" floor is the highest guest floor, though, as the owners live in one tower and the other is full of construction material. The hotel's predecessor had a proper fourth story above this one, but due to constraints of time and cost, reconstruction stopped here.

I follow the front hallway south, paralleling South Main, then turn right. 205 is towards the rear of the building, on the left side of the hallway; it's one of the economy rooms overlooking Gates Street. I let myself in with a skeleton key, a particularly worn, scratched skeleton key, marred from untold years riding in pockets with other keys and jangling none too delicately in this brass lock. The door swings open on a "dormitory style" hostel room, with an empty white book case on the right, white metal coat rack leaning perilously in the corner, faded yellow chair, old and worn wooden desk with a matching stool, a towel rack over a trash can, separate faucets for hot and cold water in a sink under a chipped mirror, one low radiator in the corner...

This room seems more historically authentic than 105—more accessible to the everyday traveler and railroad worker than the comparably opulent front rooms. The walls are light cream, marked here and there with nail holes and chips, a crack running several feet skyward at a stark angle, a water stain on the ceiling above the sink. The brown carpet is pocked with indentions from the furniture legs.

Then there is the heart of the room, the surprisingly large queen size bed with a blue top sheet, two pillows, and a view from the mattress of the peeling paint atop the Miller Pontiac/Chevrolet/Cadillac dealership across the street. One light hangs overhead, matched in function by a table lamp and a corner lamp, though matched in function alone—the former has a pink shade, the latter, a dirty brown fabric shade.

A box fan hides under a dark-stained desk, its mate in the corner by the door standing four drawers tall under five gleaming faux brass coat hooks. Nothing matches here, but everything works—aside from the blinds over one of the two windows, which slope precipitously towards the floor, the slats bent, twisted in the afternoon sunlight playing coyly over their bones. This is a working man's dormitory. This is a railroad man's hotel room.

This is what the hotel used to offer, and at that, more than most men needed. If anything, it personifies White River Junction's industrial spirit: the accoutrements function, and they are spaced efficiently. There are two sprinklers overhead for safety, and a solid floor below. Minimal concessions are made for comfort, though several—two desks, plenty of lighting—are made for function...just what a no-nonsense man needs when he places his pocket watch upon the desk and hangs his suit for a short night's respite. The view through dirty windows— their coating of dust glows this afternoon—is of commerce, industry, history: the oldest continuously running family-owned Cadillac dealership in the world.

Beyond that roof, through the trees, I see The Hill. Many captains of industry built their homes on The Hill, physically above the commercial hubbub below. There, several degrees above the horizon, was something to look up to from this working room: comfortable elegance earned through hard work and smart dealing. The front rooms are nice, but this is the sort of room rented to the folks who built the town; that view shows the workingman's dream during White River Junction's heyday. 205, this low-rent, functional room, is the soul of this hotel.

* * * * *

Back at the top of the stairs I face a choice: I could go down to the lobby, investigate a locked glass door that leads directly into the adjacent building, or walk left towards the hostel rooms; I go left, leaving the carpet for varnished wood. I follow the grain of the hardwood floor west, walking between hostel rooms 221 on my left, then 220 across the hall, the numbers counting up on the right and down on the left. There are pineapples stenciled above each doorway, and a low veneer table on the right. It bears "Hallowed Ground" and "North & South," two magazines dedicated to Civil War history. There is also a red hardcover book stamped "SEP 17 1931," with the title <u>An Introduction to Practical Bacteriology</u>. Next to it sits a 1926 Bible in German—it is only one year older than this incarnation of the Hotel Coolidge.

The sprinkler pipe overhead runs all the way to the exit sign at the end of the hall. The floor groans with each step I take and moans with every foot I raise, saying something incomprehensible in that dead language of ancient buildings.

There is a small door in the wall just above my head, and swinging it open—on oiled hinges—I see eight glass electrical fuses. This solid door really should be replaced with glass, the metal frame with a decorative wooden one, to show off the yellow- and blue-circled antique glass fuses—industrial art. Likely, they're still in use.

A Center for Cartoon Studies worker lives at the end of the hallway, in 216—but the 1 on the door has been blacked out with a marker. He is Rich Temeso, an artist working with the Center's Director, James Sturm. Last week I met him in Inky's, where he looked cautiously up from a graphic novel and said "the people here are really nice," then awkwardly added a moment later, "I really like living here." He is a man of few words.

Across the hall, the frame around door 215 slopes hazardously down and to the right. The door itself is cut so the upper right corner forms a matching slope, the effect of which could throw you off were it not for the matching slope of the floor falling away from the bottom of the door. The doorway, then, is rhomboidal.

The wood floor here in the "hostel" changes color from dark brown to an industrial gray that looks like wet cement. To the right is a tile-floor bathroom with a five-loop radiator, single commode, and a shower added well after original construction. The hallway bends around load-bearing posts hidden behind walls, curving with the flow of new construction past a kitchenette on the left. The door to this room was carved through a wall, the new doorjamb of which perfectly blocks use of an old door that would presumably open into dormitory room 216.

This really strikes me—beside the doorjamb is quite obviously another door, one which can no longer possibly open; especially given the ancient steel lock that secures its latch to the wall. The old door is six inches shorter than the new one, suggesting a time when buildings were smaller for convenience of construction, design, and heating.

This was clearly not a part of the old opulent front area; lower cost rooms back here welcomed lower class customers. The Hotel Coolidge had agreements with the Railroad until the 1980s for their workers to stay in these rooms and use these facilities. That changed with the times, and now the few railroaders who need to sleep in White River Junction visit the motels by the interstate.

With that room behind me now, I walk the twisting halls and find more showers—in a dedicated shower room—to my right, and to my left a living room with padded chairs, two rectangular tables, and a padded couch. Some of the chairs match, and the bench matches the table, but nothing matches the green padded chair below the wall-mounted television. A kitchen at one end has the bare necessities for cooking: a stove, microwave, toaster, and shelves for communal storage of spices, oils, and flour. The lone refrigerator houses other staples of young hostel dwellers' diets: orange juice, jelly, and Kraft American cheese in individual plastic wrappers. The accommodations are quite plush considering one's basic needs, and everything is clean, in good repair, and inviting—that the furniture doesn't match is hardly relevant back here.

Farther down the hall, past "The World History Chart" screwed into the wall, I follow the overhead sprinkler pipes to the fire escape-come-rear-entrance, the doors along this hall labeled with letters—O, P, S, R—instead of numbers. One is a storage room, another appears lived in, the spaces within maximized with vertical stacks and dense piles of decorations, bed frames, and other hostel equipment. The halls are well lit, the wet-cement-looking wooden floor glistening below crystalline light fixtures.

I walk back along the hallway to the door of an interior, service-style stairway leading down through the walls. Each step creaks differently. I follow the signs leading to the "Self Serve Laundry," arriving on the "first floor" and wandering just beyond the commercial laundry that services the hotel. The laundry room for those living here is painted purple, with a headless golden mop handle below a dedication: "The Golden Mop is a posthumous award to anyone overflowing the washer." The next door is the hotel maintenance office with a sign Scotch-taped in place that says "What Ever."

Sadly, it reflects the attitude taken by too many previous owners, as over the years some important creaks have gone ignored in the cacophony of old-building complaints. When David Briggs purchased the Hotel Coolidge in 1984, it had been under the ownership or management of around a dozen previous entities from private citizens to distant corporations. They left their marks on the hotel, for good and ill. The 1925 reconstruction made this building into a 160 guest room hotel, but subsequent remodeling combined rooms and added amenities to render the current 53 room floor plan. This reflected the changing times, coming in the late 1940s under Zollikofer, during the decline in importance and use of the Central Vermont and Boston & Maine railroads for passenger service. It was nearly impossible to fill all of the rooms—or even a hundred of them—so walls came down to make the rooms larger and more inviting.

When all passenger service ceased in 1964, the state stretched a ten-foot tall chain link fence between the railroad right-of-way and the town. Their rationale was that, without passengers needing to disembark, there was no need for access to the tracks, and a fence would make things safer. The railroad workers who still needed access to the Hotel Coolidge and to town could go around the fence, they presumed. That unsightly metal fence officially cut the hotel off from its lifeblood, leaving it to fend for itself against chain motels closer to the thoroughfares.

Travelers through White River Junction arrived then as they do now, by private automobile on the new interstate or by taking the bus. Local residents, passing through from Quechee or Hanover, West Lebanon or Norwich, usually return home without needing to stay at the hotel. Those who need a place to stay often settle for an easy option along the interstate without ever discovering the Hotel Coolidge.

"This is not the only choice for the traveling sales people," Briggs said. "They choose the chains because they know what they're getting. They like the benefits." Until recently, the Hotel Coolidge was not listed on hotel reservation internet sites; even with an internet presence now, the less expensive motels with cheap breakfast bars and "loyalty clubs" lure travelers away. What they miss in well-lit corridors lined with identical doors leading to identical rooms, in hotels built from concrete and standard blueprints, is the rich history and adventure of an authentic landmark—they miss local flavor in the places they visit.

Each room here has its own character, from the hostel dormitories to the opulent front rooms, President Coolidge's Parlor Room A to room 205, the mix of old and new...the adventure through time along the corridors, listening to the boards creaking, smelling the history and wondering who could have stayed here before. The difference is that between water and wine.

* * * * *

The Hotel Coolidge is planted firmly in the present,

in the most basic way that all things which currently exist are present right now. It honors the past as well, from architecture that evokes the Junction Houses before it, to its very name, and looks to the future through David Briggs' eyes. What has been a stop for the affluent, the working class, Presidents and paupers, is now available to students and leaf peepers and anyone else who needs a hotel or hostel room.

There are heavy wooden beams from the 1920s, a mural from the 1950s, magazines from the 1990s... this hotel does not belong to one specific time, nor one specific demographic. Its historical schizophrenia is somehow congruous, and familiar in ways you might not expect—and won't soon forget. David's efforts to preserve history are gallant, and refreshing in how—by accident or design, I cannot tell—he allows the hotel to interweave modern art (the Zollikofer gallery) and young cartoon art students with the hotel's carefully preserved heritage. If anything, this keeps the eighty year old hotel with a century and a half's history allied with modernity.

With these thoughts in mind I walk across the first floor, down the stairs to the lobby, and turn my key in again at the front desk. "I was beginning to wonder what you were up to," the receptionist says, relieved. I thank her and turn towards the plate glass windows facing onto South Main Street. Workers in jeans and old coats bustle past with their collars turned up against the October chill, the sun long set while I was discovering the Hotel Coolidge. The modern world outside this parlor doesn't look very inviting, at least not compared to the warm glow in the fireplace, the comfortable couches, the comforting air that smells like old stories and new smoke. But it is time for me to turn the page and close this chapter; I step through the breezeway and onto the sidewalk, where the night air smells like smoke and change.

The Junction—The confluence of the White River (flowing right to left) and the Connecticut River (flowing left to right). Trains crossed into New Hampshire here. To the photographer's right is the railroad bridge heading north, farther into Vermont. Harold Wright, former White River Junction Postmaster, remembers when a fair amount of mail sorting was done by hand in the cars as they were pulled along.

History in the Mail

This postcard has a door in it. Not printed on it, but an actual door in the front with a paper hinge and a small brass latch that keeps it closed. When it was printed in 1905, it cost only a few cents, and one penny to mail.

So what do you keep behind a door in a postcard? This one is made from paper pressed together in the days before cardboard, forming a small compartment around a photo accordion. The Rotograph Co. of New York City patented this design in 1905 and copyrighted the pictures inside a year later. They chose for the front, printed over the door, an overhead photograph of White River Junction, Vermont, at the turn of the twentieth century.

The photograph shows the village as a remote industrial town nestled in the Green Mountains, bordered to the north and east by the White and Connecticut rivers respectively, and filled with stout warehouses and mills. One hundred years after it was printed, the photograph still shows remarkable detail right down to the chimneys—here are houses and businesses together, a railroad line skirting the banks of two rivers, and trees lining hillsides. The details speak volumes, as details often do, but the most interesting detail is the door right in the middle of the card. Opening it, the photo accordion unfolds a street level tour of the city.

Postcards send at least two messages: the picture on

the front, and then whatever is written on the back. We collect them for both, taping them to the refrigerator or a wall and in so doing, hiding the message on the back to keep for ourselves. There are postcards that make nice decorations, and postcards you keep in a shoebox to read on rainy days. But they can also work as touchstones to the past, portals to new places, ways of keeping in touch while bringing others into your life, and of course, simple correspondence. A standard three inch by five inch postcard doesn't have much room for pictures or messages, but can say so much—their details speak volumes that can't fit in just fifteen square inches.

The pictures on this photo accordion are just around an inch square, and are remarkably clear for pressed ink lithographs on a narrow paper ribbon. The first image is St. Anthony's Catholic Church on Church Street at the divide between residential and commercial areas—between work and family life. This was an important building then, as many still find it today, its importance made clear in this—the lead—picture for whoever opened the card in Massachusetts, or New York, or Pennsylvania.

The next print is the three-story high school, and then the Episcopal Church, then one of a long covered bridge labeled redundantly "old covered bridge over White River."

Of the ten pictures, two show churches, three show businesses, two are nature scenes, two feature bridges, and one shows Wilder, a town just to the north. The prints are interesting, even though the architecture is quite similar—several of them were built under the direction of the same man, George Smith. But what they show is as important as the image itself. This postcard

86

was made to be mailed to someone the sender did not see regularly—someone who most likely lived outside of White River Junction, and might not see the city in their lifetime. What was it like, they might wonder, for their sister or son in this mountain town? What mattered there?

The accordion shows the churches that were always bustling on Sunday, the modern schoolhouse built in 1884, and that marvel of engineering, the covered bridge spanning the White River. Lest the recipient confuse this industrial town with Boston or New York City, there are two prints of beautiful nature scenes along the Connecticut River. These pictures can represent life in a town that a distant relative or friend might never see. If pictures are indeed worth a thousand words, this postcard says more than the longest letter, and still there is room on the back to write briefly about the day's business.

Letters and postcards kept families in touch before everyone had e-mail, or even telephones. At the turn of the last century, very few people could afford to own cameras or develop film—photographs were reserved for only the most important people, places, and occasions. The only way for a farmer in Virginia to understand what his nephew's city looked like in the Green Mountains was to hear him describe it in a letter, or wait for a postcard. They were treasured not just for the pictures, not just the short messages on the back, but as small views into worlds far away—worlds where their married children lived, or where the jobs were better and "you should move once I am settled," as someone wrote.

There are other postcards here in a stack loaned to me

by David Briggs, the owner of the Hotel Coolidge. I had only passing interest in postcards, but he was excited to show these off. Each has a picture or cancellation mark that has something to do with this part of Vermont where the rivers and railroads converge, and cover rather well the first thirty years of the 1900s. Atop the stack was that postcard with the door.

Not all of these postcards were mailed; some stayed in private collections. But the ones that found their ways first out of White River Junction, and then back via collector circles and internet auctions, offer fascinating pictures of life well before our time. Each one is its own little door into the past.

Alma V Ernest was still new to town when she wrote to her siblings on November 14, 1915, about her new life. On the back of a postcard addressed to Mrs. William Russell, Lisbon, NH, she wrote:

> Dear Sister and Brother, We like here quite well. Have been to see where they are building the Mill this afternoon. E. say to tell Bill this is going to be home when the Mill gets started. I have a down stairs tenement and like very much. We have a lovely church. Tell Emma I will send her a card later. Alma V Ernest.

The card she selected shows the town from overhead, colored in beautiful pastel as a miniature of a painting done from a photograph. The artist captured the railroad trestle and dirt streets in just the right light to make the city look comfortable, peaceful—the sort of place you should be glad your sister lives.

But then there are the unsettling postcard pictures

of floods, washed out bridges, and damage from The Hurricane of 1938. Here is a photograph of a man rowing quietly through placid waters past a Bridge Street sign jutting defiantly above the water. He rows past houses during the March 19, 1936 flood that washed out several buildings. A yellowed brown-and-white photo from March 4, 1927 shows a similar scene of water where streets should be, the crest lapping at windowpanes. With dramatic pictures of White River Junction at its best, why would postcard companies print pictures of the town at its worst? It strikes me odd that there is a market for postcard pictures of one's hometown submerged in river water to mail to concerned friends and family.

But this was front page news, and easier to mail than a newspaper. Would family members higher in the mountains know what floods look like? And if postcards keep distant relations abreast of current events, then why not show catastrophe when it happens? If they are valuable for recording the places and events of importance, the catastrophic has as much claim as the wonderful. There is space on the back to write that the family is safe, after all.

These catastrophe postcards also show the development of bridges across the White River and into the town of Hartford. A magnificent covered bridge was built between the towns in 1868. It is the bridge featured on the photo accordion, and also on several later postcards that show it washed up on the riverbank. It met its fate in March of 1913, when a severe flood raised the river to unprecedented levels. More than two and a half million feet of logs were held in a pen above the town awaiting the annual log drive to mills downstream when the flood waters swept them away. They smashed like torpedoes against the covered bridge until it slipped its foundation and washed ashore.

One postcard shows the bridge head-on, with its warning sign clearly visible. It reads: "moving faster than a walk positively forbidden autos go slow danger," an unpunctuated warning that kept the bridge safe from predictable failure until the unprecedented calamity.

This bridge was replaced with a metal bridge, and several postcards deeper in the stack is a view from the riverbank on the White River Junction side that shows its first few feet of steel thrust longingly into thin air— it was washed away as well. Of the whole stack, only three postcards show photographs of the town within the last twenty years; one of them—near the bottom of the pile—shows the concrete Interstate 91 bridge high over the White River. It has not washed away, and is so high above the town that it likely never will. These bridge photos chronicle the accomplishments of laborers who toiled with wood and nails and steel over a gurgling river; they show the awesome power of nature destroying first one bridge and then a second and improved bridge, and the triumph of today's construction over that vengeful water; they show the importance of bridges, and the indomitable spirit of the townspeople. Set side by side they are quite remarkable—a chronicle of accomplishments and calamities, their stories interwoven with the town and preserved here in this mailable history.

As stories are interrelated in small towns, so are other postcards in this stack. The painting on Mrs. Ernest's 1915 card shows the exact view over the Junction House hotel, centered on the trestle, as was captured in a photograph on another postcard. That black and white print is labeled "View From Barron's Point," and indeed it shows everything a twentieth century baron could want in a city: modern industrial buildings, railroad lines for bringing in supplies and shipping goods out to market, a church, rivers that power mills... There is a fancy border stamped around the card where wet dies embossed ridges onto the paper, framing the picture handsomely and giving the fingers something to feel.

Mr. Tony Linsmper of "Ethan Ave, Westfield, Mass," received this particular postcard. Whoever sent it placed the green one-cent stamp upside down and mailed it without signing his name. In fact, Mr. Linsmper's street address is missing as well—a tiny detail that spins the brass latch on another door to his bygone era.

Few of the cards give street names, and even fewer list house numbers. Addresses like "Miss Mamie Huffard, Hancock, Vermont," and "Miss Helen Paull, Myrichs, Mass," were sufficient. They were delivered in the days of true small-town-America, when the postman knew everyone on his route. The Post Office began delivering mail to homes when Ohio postal clerk Joseph Briggs came up with the idea during the Civil War. 1896 saw the first rural delivery of mail to farms and homesteads across the country, linking families like never before. The streets were short, the country roads were long, and confusion was rare...even in such cases as with White River Junction's two Robert Smiths—father and son. Post Masters knew just about everyone in town, and just about everyone in town knew their neighbors. Should two men from Montpelier have met on the platform at White River Station they might indeed discover a common acquaintance, if they did not recognize each other immediately. It makes sense that writing a name and a city was all one needed to address a postcard. Times were simpler.

So were the postcards. Most of them feature a single picture, rendered in black and white on sturdy cardstock. The exceptions include stunning color prints, originally black and white photos but with pastel colors added later.

Early offset printing presses in Germany, where many of these cards were printed as per the printers' stamps, used color to add almost a third dimension to the photographs. The most startling example is in two pictures looking north along West Main Street (called North Main Street these days). In the black and white photograph a dirt road extends into the distance, the ruts from carriage wheels and thin tires leading your eyes out of town, under the sign for Miss M. McCabe Millinery and past the Smith & Son confectionery across the street. The signs are legible and the picture is straightforward, if a little bland coming as it has after paintings of the town and dramatic photos of individual buildings.

Then I turn to the colorized photo—the exact same picture, but presented with the benefit of soft brown, green, and blue. Like a few years' perspective brings history into clearer focus, the colors here bring the picture vividly to life. The signs are easier to read for the contrast, hidden details sprout up like springtime grass, and it looks like you should feel the grain of the boards as you rub your finger over the picture. What a difference a little color can make!

And what a difference a little time can make. Only one of the businesses on the postcards is still operational:

the Hotel Coolidge. Some of the buildings themselves are gone, lost to fire like the second White River Station and the Smith & Son confectionery building. Were it not for the picture of West Main Street with the confectionery on a corner I recognize today, I might not have known what a magnificent brick building stood there before the current used furniture store and salon. Moreover, without this vivid postcard, I might not have cared.

And if they do little else for us today, if knowing what used to be where before and why is irrelevant to the here and now, then at least postcards make us care; at least they give us those portals to other places, other lives, and other times. There is no bringing back the Twin State Fruit Co. from across the tracks by the modern courthouse, but there is something special in the feeling you get looking back through a hundred years at a town you know, in a form you'll never see firsthand. What once brought White River Junction, warm greetings, and welcome news to friends far beyond the town now brings those same messages far beyond their time.

This is what those deceptively simple postcards can do for us. Spin the latch, open the door...and take a little trip.

Tip Top Building—As seen from the railroad tracks where boxcars formerly lined up to haul away Smith and Sons' Hanover Crackers. These windows—still featuring their manufacturers' stickers—are part of the renovations that created the Tip Top Media Building from its former self.

After The Empire
White River Junction seen through the Tip Top Building's Windows

An overcast sky hangs low, form-fitting and heavy like a death shroud over White River Junction today, making it a good afternoon to stay indoors. These streets I drive are lined with large buildings cobbled together from smaller ones, former alleys turned into hallways behind new bricks that don't quite match the old. The only other cars on North Main Street are bound in the opposite direction—out of town. It's hard to see, but new life stirs behind the historic façades of the sleepy mountain village around me; some of them, anyway, and today I'm in search of a good example. Artists who call old buildings "art historical" have taken over the fire station at 58 Bridge Street, a ground floor shop in the Gates Block, established the Center for Cartoon Studies in the Colodny Building on South Main, and taken over an old bakery here on North Main. They create progressive art in classic buildings, drawing electric inspiration from their surroundings like magnets running over copper wires. A number of them rent studio space in the bakery, a quirky building whose story is that of the town; once the center of an empire that shaped White River Junction, now it just might be ground zero for the town's rebirth. I turn into its parking lot, passing a small sign that reads "Tip Top

Media," searching for hope.

A Vermont state quarter locked in the concrete at the threshold displays the year 2001 and a scene where a man gathers maple sap from his trees. Welcome to Vermont; we have syrup. A hundred years ago that quarter might have shown this building and a box of Hanover Crackers—this old bakery produced them by the tens of millions, financing an empire whose fate was interwoven with that of this town, and one family. But that was a long time ago, and this 21st century coin in the threshold welcomes you to the new era. I open the glass double doors into the Tip Top Building and step inside a bold new world.

Green pipes, red floors, silver paint, posters flapping on bricks...someone else's dinner wafting out from the Tip Top Café, dust and Lysol...these things hit me at once. No potion available over the counter packs quite the wallop as your first entrance into the Tip Top Building.

There is no sound save the doors swooshing closed behind me, though in a place this vibrant there should be. There needs to be a Tip Top Sound complementing the sights and smells; sometimes there is one, as party music and laughter spill out of the Tip Top Café during costume parties. Everything is silent now, though; everything needs to rest sometime.

Below the dinner smells are those yellow and brown, clay smells from the Tip Top Pottery studio where Anthologie used to be. Anthologie: an "antiquarian, used, and first edition books" store, and something of a time capsule in second hand literature, used to be here just inside the front doors; it was appropriate that the new business sold old books in the freshly renovated

96

historical building. Many businesses passed through here, and something will replace the pottery studio in time.

The walls don't match the pipes or the floor or each other, but the colors work very well together and with the impressionist paintings and life size sculptures. Artifacts from the Tip Top's past are displayed everywhere. The central hallway extends before me, branching to the left and right with a T-intersection at the far end. Each hallway is a trip through White River's history and the collective consciousness of the forty different artists and creative professionals who lease office space under the Tip Top's silver roof.

Extending beyond the entryway is the Hall Of Industrial Antiquities (HOIA), an artistic exhibition of objects once familiar to the building. Twenty some paces from the front door stands the first exhibit, a vertical display of bricks and tile—words fallen from the pages of time. Industrial history is the primary theme linking squashed baseballs, rusty metal, wood fragments, and other pieces of "found art." David Fairbanks Ford, the curator of the Main Street Museum and artistic contributor to the HOIA, explains in a small sign that such exhibits in historic spaces around White River Junction

> create a public space where objects can be critically analyzed through multiple disciplines—utilizing not only traditional methods of art historical, scientific and qualitative criticism, but sociological and even psychological analysis as well. Responsivity in artifacts offers a means of access to their

sometimes hidden inner-lives.

The collection in the HOIA is as eccentric as the building; the Tangled Things section features steel wires and braided metal that is, quite obviously, tangled. The "Oxidation" section, displaying a theme repeated throughout the hall, features rusty metal. What art is there in a deteriorating metal spike in a crumbling gold-painted frame? In another sign, Ford calls it all "Evidence of Deconstruction in the Construction and Carpentry Trades." In the Vermont Standard newspaper, he explained "it's not so much the object as the reaction to it that's important." Just as the railroad spikes rust and disintegrate right there before you, the dilapidated frame falls slowly apart on the wall. There is no better frame for that display, and as it shows the industrial might of the city disintegrating before you, perhaps it is the most poignant installation in the Hall.

There is something of a baroque streak in all this—the notion that imperfections in the fabric of life remind us we're alive, and that living is only one stage everything goes through. The railroad spikes rust away before our eyes, crumbling towards oblivion like the sagging buildings along Railroad Row. They at once provide a tangible link to the glorious past of bustling commerce, and also a reminder that nothing lasts forever—neither glory nor ignominy. The tangled wires and metal hanging from the ceiling invoke a sense that buildings, workers, and now each of us in the Tip Top Media Building, are interwoven in the town's complex history; observation is a participatory act, after all.

What appears to be junk, and anywhere else would, in fact, be junk, comes alive as part of this vibrant space.

Most striking among the odds and ends is a sealed box of thick, round crackers, stacked atop and beside each other in an inverted mound set sideways. "I constructed a cracker tunnel," Ford explained, "one that would be made if you were eating your way out of a massive, life threatening pile of crackers that had been dumped on your head." Looking into the tunnel invokes a trip from the surreal HOIA corridor back in time to a small bakery five miles away in Hanover, New Hampshire.

* * * * *

The Symnes family opened a bakery in Hanover in 1815. Their most popular items were Hanover Crackers, disk shaped unleavened affairs that went well with milk or soup. They baked for the local area, with limited distribution, enjoying sufficient success to maintain the business and attract the eye of Everett Smith. Smith purchased the bakery in 1837, renamed it the Smith Bakery, and added the production of various confections he called Dartmouth Chocolate—named for Dartmouth College just a few doors up the street.

Everett's family welcomed a son, George Williston, in 1841. George grew up with the successful business, and at fifteen he joined the Smith Bakery as a traveling salesman and representative of his father's brand. He hitched up the family's delivery wagon and toured the Upper Valley taking and filling orders. He learned the basics of baking and business, supply and demand, and became a full partner in the bakery in 1867—at twenty six years old. While the family positioned itself as a prominent supplier of baked goods, White River Junction carved its place in Upper (Connecticut River)

Valley commerce with blasting caps and steel trestles—the railroad was coming to town.

In 1871 E.K. Smith & Sons bakery bid a sweet farewell to Hanover, leaving behind a town too cloistered to hold Everett's ambitions. They invested the profits from thirty-four years of business into a new, two story brick bakery and confectionery near the corner of Bridge Street and Main. It became the Smith family's toehold as they climbed the ranks of White River Junction's business elite...and became the cracker crumb cornerstone of an empire.

Ten years later, in 1881, George Smith launched the White River Paper Company out of an office below the family bakery. His business partners, Alma and S.L. Farman, were likely cursed—they brought immediate catastrophe to the bakery: a fire broke out just after the new business opened. The *Landmark* recorded the disaster, saying "Farman has moved into the basement and as he has been burned out in business three times and his house once, all inside of six years, it is safe to say the bakery 'must go' sometime."

Productivity dipped, but the bakery remained open and the White River Paper Company moved into a new Smith-owned building across the street. A fire at the bakery in 1884 lead to more renovations and the construction of a three story facility, stables for the company's teams of delivery horses, and sundry other buildings and facilities related to the expanding enterprise. Renovations and expansion reshaped E.K. Smith & Sons, expanding their conquest of the railroad right of way along their loading docks. The trains that transformed White River Junction rumbled mere feet from the facility; George Smith depended upon them for wholesale ingredients and delivery of finished products to far flung markets.

While the Smiths developed their area of Railroad Row, George also had his eye on building the town's resources to sustain his employees and the other workers who flocked to the boomtown. Driving through the modern streets of White River Junction, the keen observer can discern matching brick on buildings used in the Smith & Sons bakery, the Mascoma Bank building (formerly the First National Bank of White River Junction), the Library, the High School, and various other structures. A philanthropist as well as a shrewd businessman, Smith saw the benefits of building a community to sustain the businesses that, in turn, built the community. By 1890 George Smith owned the "Smith Block" buildings, was a charter member and president of the First National Bank of White River Junction, built two schools, and established the Masonic Temple.

His bakery expanded its facilities and workforce to operate twenty four hours a day, producing enormous quantities of their signature crackers. William H. Tucker's 1889 <u>History Of Hartford</u> gives an astonishing account of their achievement:

> As an illustration to the extent of Mr. Smith's cracker making, it may be said that his annual production is 1,625,000 dozens. If this number were placed in a pile of twenty five feet square, and 113 feet in height, sixty men could stand side by side around such a pile and if each man should eat three dozen daily until the entire lot was consumed, the pile would last

30 years. He annually converts from thirty to forty carloads of flour of choice brands into 'Hanover' crackers, in what business he also uses at least 300 barrels of lard. He now makes 65,000 crackers daily, or about 50 barrels."

These crackers found their way by foot, horse drawn carriage, and railcar across the Upper Valley, New York, Massachusetts, and undoubtedly to points the Smiths themselves had never traveled. Boxcars pulled directly up to their loading docks. Pipes ran through the walls so shortening could be pumped directly from tanker cars into the bakery; everything in their increasing community of purpose-built facilities was designed for high output.

George added his son, Robert E. Smith, to the family business and changed the company name to George W. Smith & Son. Though the business named evolved, their Hanover Crackers retained their trademark name…and popularity. The Smiths purchased the Vermont Baking Company and moved its production into a steam laundry building Smith owned, securing their prosperity through the close of the 19th century. White River Junction was in full growth and its brick skin bore the indelible legacy of George and Robert Smith.

Robert later simplified the company name to Smith & Son, leading the business into the 20th century. Their product line included cigars, candy, chocolate, Hanover Crackers, and other goods produced in a complicated series of buildings that relied expressly on the adjacent railroad for supplies and distribution. Rumors about their business ethics persist; some were voiced in the "Trains" issue of the Hartford area *Electric Organ*. Those rumors claimed that "monopoly, price fixing and gouging... coercion at both the retail and wholesale markets, corporate looting, and the sometimes violent quelling of workplace organization" facilitated the Smith family's success. Few empires avoid such allegations, and strong sentiment towards the Smith family—for good and for ill—lingers even today.

Despite the allegations he suffered, Robert Smith received acclaim for continuing the family legacy of social leadership. He became the president of the First National Bank, the president of the Inter-State Trust Company, a Director of the Passumpsic and Connecticut River division of the Boston & Maine railroad, a member of the New England Telephone and Telegraph Co. Advisory Board, a Director of the Ottauquechee Woolen Co., and the chairman of the town's Board of Selectmen. I presume he also found time to sleep, though certain parties claim that would have been accomplish upside down in the Evangelical Church's bell tower.

Smith & Sons kept their costs low by purchasing ingredients by the trainload, owning their facilities and land, and commanding such export volume as to control a dominant share of any distributor's business—a formidable bargaining tool. The iron grip they maintained over the company, and over White River Junction's financial infrastructure, entwined their private prosperity with that of the city—just like the twisted wires in the Tangled Things exhibit, one hundred years later in the heart of their former empire.

Robert Smith fathered two sons, George W. II and Robert W. II, during the height of Smith & Son's early 20th century success. In 1915 he erected a large building on North Main for the Vermont Baking Company. Adjacent to this production hub was the sprawling complex of the Smith & Son bakery, confectionery, livery, and the loading docks that kept the family business humming. More than three hundred workers formed three daily shifts, many living in Smiths' tenement houses across the street. The *Electric Organ* observed, "one really couldn't say whether the company was located in the town or that the town resided within the jurisdiction of the omnipotent factory."

World War I was the turning point for politics, science, and economies in several countries, in a conflict that affected every family in America and Europe. The Smiths, despite their affluence, could not escape the national supply pinch and the very personal cost of sending George W. II and Robert W. II to war. The brothers received Army officer commissions and served while their father tended the family businesses. In 1917, Robert E. Smith contracted aciatic rheumatism and passed away in a railroad car in Burlington, Vermont. Robert's funeral was attended by virtually the entire town, from the workers who arrived "in a block," to the town's vanguard of business and social leaders.

Their figurehead, the latest embodiment of the Smith legacy, was laid to rest...along with much of the town's progressive energy. His pallbearers were, with the exception of a single man, the same who bore his father's coffin in 1905. With the sons away for military service, proprietorship of Smith & Son defaulted to an uncle, Asa B. Hebard. The momentum of the Smith enterprises, building exponentially from the Symnes bakery in Hanover, slowed as if out of respect for the deceased...and never regained its speed.

George returned to the business in 1919, his brother

in 1921, and they struggled to hold the steady course their family charted since 1837. The war years were not kind to the business or the brothers' command of the financial monolith, and in 1923 they sold the Vermont Baking Company to the facility's manager, George C. West. George W. II stepped into his father's former role as the president of the First National Bank and the Director of the Interstate Trust Company, ultimately becoming a senior partner in Smith, Batchelder, Smith, Rugg & Darling Certified Public Accountants.

Smith & Son continued to operate into the Great Depression, when money for food was scarce and customers could ill afford confections. They increased their focus on local distribution, adding an automobile garage to maintain a fleet of delivery vehicles. Ultimately they fought a losing battle in an era that swallowed regional businesses amidst crippling national poverty.

In 1934, the Smith family resigned themselves to ignominious defeat. They closed Smith & Son and abandoned their enterprise. Their buildings were taken over by other, far less prosperous businesses. Most sat vacant. The money that poured into the Smith family's coffers ceased, and so too did the philanthropic projects that built the town. The offering plate at the Smith's church lightened, and the town awoke to an age where unemployed workers could not infuse local stores and landlords with cash. Money flows through societies like water, from employers to workers, to landlords and retailers and shopkeepers who redistribute it again to more workers. One of the prominent pools from which this cycle drew life dried up behind the closed doors of the defunct bakery.

* * * * *

The Vermont Baking Company, under George C. West, survived the Great Depression just yards from the failed Smith enterprises. They continued production through World War II, until George sold it to the Ward Baking Co. in 1945. Sometime thereafter the Ward Baking Co. erected a 100 ton flour tower in their facility, which today is an elevator shaft. Through annexation and the practice of renovating existing structures rather than razing them and building anew, the Ward Baking Co. grew to encompass the former Smith & Sons buildings.

Named for Ward's Tip Top Bread, they coined their facility the Tip Top Building. The adjacent bakeries, garages, stables, and other spaces were patched together with masonry until one large building dominated the railroad right of way. Walls in certain hallways formerly kept out the fierce New England winters; now they divide compartments in the coalesced structure.

On the eastern face of their building, Ward painted the endearing—and enduring—advertisement of a girl unwrapping a loaf of Tip-Top Bread, with the slogan "It's like opening the door to a bakery." The girl's faded ghost still smiles down on the rails that brought her bread to the country, but a window cut into the wall somewhat fittingly replaced the word "door."

They attempted new construction in the 1970s when, amidst accusations of economically strong-arming the city, they convinced officials to sell the municipal parking lot adjacent to the Tip Top. Ward argued that expanding the bakery could produce more jobs and revenue to fight the city's economic decay. The city acquiesced, and Ward built a metal building to enclose 5,000 square feet of usable space. The next year, they closed the entire facility and Ward left White River Junction completely.

Businesses left for new shipping hubs around the interstates, or across the river in West Lebanon, New Hampshire. After the transportation revolution and the decline of railroad-centric commerce, New Hampshire's lower state taxes and a lack of sales tax on most goods stole away the last good reasons to operate in White River Junction. The exodus packed up the town's last hopes and fading glory, taking to the highways and leaving brick and mortar integuments crumbling along Railroad Row. The Tip Top building changed hands, its various interior spaces rented to sundry businesses ranging from Tip Top Tire to a convenience store, a taxi cab service to various artists seeking studio lofts.

One tenant was a rehabilitation center focused on turning around lives in a city many considered to be itself beyond salvation. The roof leaked. Neglect steadfastly rotted charm into eyesore. An unscrupulous owner stripped the fixtures and fittings from the building for resale as scrap. White River Junction fell hard upon its nadir.

Observing the town before I look behind the scenes, into the buildings and through the records, I got the impression that not much happens during the day—that life in White River Junction had ebbed with history's tides and was just about gone. There is always an empty seat in the Polka Dot Diner—usually a great number of empty seats—and never much traffic on Main Street. It's even quieter at night.

But then I looked more closely. Some of the bones

glowed with what could be, perhaps by a miracle, an ember of reanimation's fire. The fight against entrenched stagnation comes not with a mason's trowel, but a painter's brush; less the workman's sweat on worn floorboards, more the paint and plaster splashed across canvas and walls. Several puppeteers plot behind the scenes to rattle the town back to life; they are friends with the painters, dramatists, cartoonists, sculptors, alternative medicine healers, and a few artistic developers who moved in while the rent was low.

One is Matt Bucy, architect, videographer, puppeteer, and the current owner of the Tip Top Building. The other is David Fairbanks Ford, a friend of Bucy's in the tight knit art world alive and growing in these quiet old buildings; Ford renovated the old fire station into the esoteric Main Street Museum and collaborated on the renovations to the Tip Top Building.

Bucy purchased the Tip Top Building in 2000 after becoming infatuated with the idea a year before. He searched White River Junction for a place to develop a studio for his visual art, namely filmmaking, and came to the Tip Top to inquire about leasing space. Across the street from a Verizon telecommunications hub, the building is perfectly situated for internet developers and other information technology companies; imbued with a century of local history, it is an ideal creative space for artists. Rather than rent a room, the owners suggested he buy the whole thing. A year later he closed the deal and set about reversing decades of neglect.

There comes a voice behind me, pulling me forward through the years and away from the cracker display in the Hall of Industrial Antiquities. It's Matt Bucy, who this afternoon is kind enough to share his time and show me around the Tip Top. We walk out of the HOIA, stopping on a red floor made from wooden slats that run diagonally. One wall is painted metallic silver, highlighting the tiny bumps and chinks, cracks and chips from long forgotten accidents. I run my hands over the wall, reading a Braille history of the men who passed daily with loads of bread and carts of flour. Did anyone finish their shift and lean heavily against this exact spot, considering where their future was going just as I look back and wonder where the building has been?

Matt explains that we just exited one of the formerly individual buildings, and how the wooden floor is an original loading dock. Down the hall, towards the railroad tracks beyond the rear exit, is Holmquist Furniture. They custom craft fine furniture in a livery building that was erected by George W. Smith in the 1880s. This hallway was built between three existing buildings; its inside walls formerly kept New England winters outside the bakery. In the context of contrasting colors and mixing history, this all seems so natural.

Matt's vision for the building is to "cater to creative businesses, to artists," he says. An artist working in several media himself, Matt embraced the opportunity to bring a historical building back to life and infuse it with the soul of White River Junction's emerging art community. "I was surprised to see so many healers," he says of the therapists and healing arts specialists in the building, adding that he welcomes their positive addition to the community. It makes sense, though, that they would flock to a town so in need of healing; never mind that the rent is cheap.

Renovating the facility, I gather from his stories on our walking tour, was a few man hours and about $3.25

109

short of unbelievable. Previous tenants and owners left the building trashed, rusty, leaking...and full of treasure. "In the basement we have some of the original hitching gear for the horses from the stable," he says, describing an amazing find. Among the tons of debris from Tip Top Tire, the convenience store, a former motor reconditioning business, and other transient establishments, he and David Ford discovered more "found art" than either the HOIA or the Main Street Museum could hold. They took the most meaningful of the pieces, preserving them carefully (Ford is an art historian and restoration specialist), and cleared the debris for studio space. Matt sealed half of the building for the initial work, displacing the few artists who were already renting space. Artists brought canvas and clay to life while Matt, David and friends returned the Smith & Sons facility from the dead. After a year of intense work with many hired renovators, the artists moved into the finished spaces and the process began anew on the other side.

The elevator runs through the space formerly occupied by Ward's hundred ton flour tower. Matt used translucent plastic panels to enclose the shaft. Hints of the steel framework beckon from behind the plastic, giving the impression that one can see into the elevator itself. Step inside, though, and you are in a plain steel box. Close the doors and you may as well be in any office building anywhere in America. Yet, looking at the elevator from the outside, you cannot shake the feeling that there could be someone inside looking right back at you.

I get the same sense walking through the rest of the building, where I see the rise and fall of White

River Junction in the structure itself and the many artistic displays of antiquity. For all the historical touchstones—the Hall of Industrial Antiquities, various displays, Matt's running narrative, the feel of a century-old wall—I sense how much of the story is lost in that barrier between ages. Perhaps the ghost of George Smith watches us here in his former empire, checking his watch, annoyed with the slowness of my step.

We come to the Cooler Gallery, where the gutted shell of the namesake cooler forms a gallery within the gallery. A spiral staircase to the roof is enclosed, kept away from the public for safety reasons, and the rubble has been cleared to present a clean floor and engaging ambiance. The halls on the second floor follow the same style of multiple contrasting colors with vivid paint on pipes, the floor, the walls, the art… Small tables hold business cards for Sue Kirincich's yoga classes, Peter Payne's Bodymind Place, various painters, assorted sculptors… there are forty artists in fifty compartmentalized spaces carved from the cavernous interiors of the conjoined buildings.

Where conveyor belts once fed bread into ovens, folks now perform yoga. In the mixing and storage rooms, artists paint their expression of beauty while observing models and cultivating moods. We pass Studio 260, where Mark Merrill creates stained glass art. Two of his paintings hang outside the studio, the Early Autumn Sunrise, and The Sunset. A small sign near the former gives his name. In the contrasting humility of twelve-point font it also boasts the price: $3,600.

We descend a stairwell and circle around to the main hallway, tracing a path through the Vermont Baking Co. building, through a formerly open space, over a loading dock and into a building from the early 1900s. Framed pictures dot the wall opposite the displays in the HOIA, and Matt points to 1920s era photographs of the Vermont Baking Co.

"That door we went in, to the second floor," he says, pointing to a patch of brick on the upper wall of the bakery, "is right here. That's where the flour tower was built." I stare at an architectural drawing of the Vermont Baking Co. façade, penned in 1910, and note the wrought iron planters, brick arches, and stained glass. Those are long gone, replaced successively by the next big thing, then the next great thing, then pried and ripped off and sold as surplus, increasing the nostalgic value of the original design with every face lift. Matt points to a plank of wood painted green, hanging on the wall. Paint is missing where original wooden letters, nailed to the sign, spelled "Bakery."

This is part of the old Vermont Baking Co. sign, he says, pointing to the sign in an old photograph. "When we found this piece they were using it as a floorboard." The pride of the company, their very name, had been removed, cut to size, flipped over and nailed into the floor. Dozens of filthy feet trampled it, damning the Vermont Baking Co.'s pride to the same ignominy as the Smith family's crumbled empire.

The fresh paint inside the Tip Top does not conceal the building's identity, does not shame the history or obscure the heritage of strong walls and stronger wills both marred by time. Rather, it plays up the details, and the sculptures and portraits on display find ways of integrating themselves into the lingering pride of Smith's construction; the artists here don't reinvent so much as they coexist with history.

112

Down a side hallway on the second floor are belt-high statues formed from what feels like solid felt. They collect lint and dust, plush chronicles of the people and pollens that breeze through. The acrylic on canvas painting "Prophecy" by Georgina Forbes hangs in the ground floor entrance way, near the gaping entrance to the HOIA's rabbit hole. A small sign explains her painting:

> I like to underpaint some seemingly random motif—color, movement, texture—that gives a dynamic interest to the composition. It may suggest meaning or evoke energy, but remains indefinite and outside specific associations with the familiar. ...I want to surprise myself, be intrigued, and perhaps hooked away beyond limitations. I want there to be inexplicable aspects of the painting that open up a larger realm of possibility, and yet I want the provocative elements of the painting to be so right, so beautiful, that they are easily embraced by the viewer...

The painting itself hangs in the foyer before a swirling realm of possibility: the history of a building, a family, a microcosm of Industrial Age America. Surprising, intriguing, the provocative history of a town encapsulated in the story of the Tip Top evokes the energy of a dynasty. A greater introduction to the Hall of Industrial Antiquity, the Tip Top, the Smiths, and White River, does not readily come to mind.

Several wires suspend a length of pipe at the far end of the hallway, near a passage out from the history and back into the present. A sign introduces it as a "Shortening pipe from the Tip Top Bakery Building painted with traces of antique shortening from the former sculpture studio of Ria Blass. 105x19cm in diameter." Ria was one of the original artists in the Tip Top Building, and worked on larger-than-life wooden sculptures in an early studio. The summer heat warmed the pipe, liquefying the congealed shortening still contained within. Occasional globs of the historic goo fell from the pipe, splattering below. This made such an impression on her, Bucy, and visitors to her 1994 gallery showing, that the pipe was removed and lovingly displayed as part of the found art deconstructing the construction of the Tip Top.

Ria's contribution to the building, an issue of the *Electric Organ* noted, is not to be overlooked. She drew regional attention to the Tip Top Building with her show in 1994. The gallery she created from a back room in the Tip Top Building had windows on three sides, a view of the adjacent railroad tracks, and the inspirational flavor of converted industrial space—leaky shortening pipe and all.

Interest swelled in White River's artistic potential, fueled that same year by the opening of the nearby Main Street Museum. Though far from a Mecca, it attracted the sort of creative individuals inspired by the transformation of industrial areas into art space in New York's SoHo, the Leather District in Boston, and elsewhere; they saw potential for such new life in White River Junction.

Around the corner and through the railroad underpass, David Ford renovated the old fire house into new museum and loft space; he operates it as a community resource, art gallery, and modern-day Hall of Wonders
114

with a unique emphasis on White River Junction's history. Vermont Salvage in the Cross-Abbott building feels its age, but shelters a successful business that leaves no room for art space...that business's eclectic contents notwithstanding. Other historic spaces, like the Hotel Coolidge, also wear their history with pride...and dedicate hallways and other spaces for showcasing the art of the New White River Junction.

But no other site, no gallery or structure or business, quite so eccentrically brings history and art together as the Tip Top Building. It is a portal at the convergence of history and modernity, and a testament to the creativity of White River Junction's next wave of immigrants—artists.

I say goodbye to Matt for the evening and retire to the bar at the Tip Top Cafe to tame my swirling thoughts. Reservations are accepted for one of their two dozen tables, but with little market for high-class eateries here, reservations are a stroke for the ego more than a necessity for dining. The stools are empty, a sad waste of a copper top bar. Then the head chef emerges from the kitchen and greets me with a hello the likes of which nearly bowl me backwards off the stool. His jocular personality fills the space below exposed rafters, ricocheting off the polished concrete walls, welcoming me to his corner of the Tip Top Building. It's nice to see such unbridled life here in White River Junction; such animation amid the stark calm and quiet.

The bartender recommends the wild mushroom bisque, which I order. What strikes me most about the soup, before I even lift the first spoonful, is a small pile of crackers by my bowl: round, unleavened crackers, the likes of which George Smith produced more than twelve million yearly. Though now produced by the Vermont Common Cracker Company in Burlington, they are faithful to the crumbs wedged deep in the building's cracks. I lift one reverently, turning it over and trying to imagine how a brick and mortar city grew from sugar, flour, shortening and rails.

Photographs of White River Junction's glory days shine down from the walls around me. The patio is ringed with silver painted radiators, an eccentricity I barely notice in context. The Rio Blanco Social Club holds occasional dance parties here, most recently a Halloween ball. The event is an annual affair for the Club, a group formed largely of artists already enjoying each others' company in the Tip Top Building. Three Halloweens ago Bucy, Ford, Bruce MacLeod and company regarded the quiet of White River as a stage ripe for grand drama, so they organized a costume parade through downtown—the empty streets were not really being used for anything more productive at the moment anyway.

The 2003 parade was such a clamorous party, so incongruous with the reclusive town, that someone called the police to report a riot. Officers found, instead, a sort of energy long missing from the darkened streets.

The artists are taking over White River Junction, slowly; they coexist with history rather than smashing it to build new empires. They kindle a new spirit, one that has no practical use for the railroad tracks—but no hostility towards them either. I exit the building, casting a long look over my shoulder. Smith & Son's legacy permeates downtown like the musty smell of this evening's rain, but there's a new spirit under the clouds.

After touring the Tip Top Building and speaking with

116

Matt, after reading Ford's signs and running my hands over the art in the hallways, after walking through one vision of White River Junction's future, the whole feel of this place has changed—the clouds seem more cocoon-like, protecting her during metamorphosis. Many years removed from the Great Depression, she feels poised at another junction—ready for a new direction full of strange new life. There are many rooms still vacant, many buildings in need of repair, but the change has begun.

Once more, though in a strange new direction, White River Junction's wheels are in motion.

the
People

Harold Wright—Farmer, family man, and Postmaster in an era when he knew just about every person, farm, and dog on his old mail carrying route.

Harold Wright
On The Verge of All Things New

"Now, you know where the VA Hospital is, there in White River, right?" he asked me through the telephone on a February morning. "You take the road there, and then it bends down around, past the gas station, and there's a tomb back there. An above ground tomb, that'll be on your right. That's our family tomb. So you follow it around, and you'll pass Wright Reservoir Road. Keep going until you see Harvey Industries on your left, then the sawmill, and a white homestead on your right with a red barn." This is how directions are given in rural Vermont by those who know the roads like the veins in the backs of their hands. "That's our homestead, park out back."

The Hartford Historical Society gave me Harold Wright's number when I mentioned my survey of Briggs's postcards—Harold is the old Post Master, they said, and suggested he could tell me more about the town; at the least, I could see an authentic Vermont family farm. I was mainly interested in the town's buildings and how they can tell human stories, sometimes as if the buildings themselves have character…but here is a real Vermont farmer, they said, with plenty of history and character of his own and ties way back to the English. Perhaps Harold could lend a face to these stories I tell about their old town, and the way rural and village life meshed not so long ago. He sounded interesting, and his voice was just as Vermont—now there's a hard adjective to describe—as I hoped for, so I packed my notebook and followed his directions to the homestead.

And it is a homestead, more than just a two-story house, more than just land; the white farmhouse sits on nearly five hundred acres, two hundred years and twelve generations of local and family history entwined. Two miles south of White River Junction with Highway 5 running right through the front yard, this is the homestead of Harold and Maxine Wright. It resembles a number of Vermont postcards—there is a barn near the home, a covered log pile, and acres of open farmland bordered by distant forests. Today is late in the winter of 2006. I sit near Harold Wright in his dining room while Maxine bakes chocolate chip cookies and a light snow falls upon the Green Mountains around us.

Harold and Maxine are the last direct descendents of the men who chartered the Town of Hartford, Vermont, way back in the days of British Colonialism. The intermediate generations came north on foot and horseback, living close to the land, working this farm and others. Their adult children work in modern White River Junction, where they can surf the internet for airline tickets to anywhere in the world.

Harold and Maxine's marriage, the union of those last lines, coincided with that paradigm shift between antiquity and this bold new modernity—between steam-powered industry and internet-enabled jet aircraft; between rural life and urban sprawl. Sitting here watching the snow fall, he introduces me to eleven generations of his family, telling their stories in the soothing voice of an old farmer surprisingly well heeled

122

in the ways of city talk.

New opportunity, upon new land, lured the Wright family from England to their current homestead in Vermont, the first leg of which Lieutenant Abel Wright of Leverton, England, undertook in the mid 1600s. He settled around Hartford, Connecticut with the wife he met in The Colonies: Martha Ketcherel. Thus began the American lineage of the Wright family, a line that stayed in Connecticut for only three generations. On July 26th, 1708, the family suffered a savage Indian attack.

Harold has a fifteen page family history that, among other anecdotes, describes how, "On July 26, 1708 seven or eight Indians rushed into the house of Lt. Abel Wright of Skipmuch in Springfield, and killed two soldiers...scalped the wife of Lt. Wright, who died Oct. 19; took Hannah, the wife of Lt. Wright's son Henry, and probably slew her; killed her infant son Henry in a cradle and knocked in the head of her daughter Hannah, aged 2 years, in the same cradle; the latter recovered."

In another part of the Connecticut Territory, the Gillett family also suffered violence from Indians' tomahawks. Joseph Gillett, Harold's great, great, great, great grandfather, was killed by Indians at Bloody Brook in Suffolk County, Massachusetts, on September 18th, 1675. Samuel Gillett was killed in an Indian battle at Turner Falls, Massachusetts, on May 19th of 1676, just a year later. The last Indian kidnapping of a Gillett happened to John on September 16th, 1696, where he was borne away to Canada, according to a hand-written entry in the Gillett family Bible made by Lieutenant Israel Gillett, John's grandson. In Canada, John was given to the employ of nuns, who sent him away to France after two years. He then embarked a ship for

England, and forwarded himself back to the Colonies, where he arrived home late in 1698, according to George Sheldon's A History of Deerfield.

I have a problem with that chronology. How can an abduction and transport—by canoe and foot—to Canada, two years employ in the service of nuns, a trans-Atlantic voyage to France, transport to England, a trans-Atlantic trip back to the Colonies, and foot transport home again to Deerfield only take two years? His employ with the nuns alone lasted two years, according to the account in A History of Deerfield...but those are the dates given by the documents. In relation to the details, this discrepancy seems minimal—whatever the time frame, it undoubtedly happened, and like most of history, the story doesn't rely on exact precision for its broader drama.

I wonder how such a traumatic separation and grueling return affected John; what changed in him during those years away? All we have are the skeletal facts and dubious dates—history tends to guard its secrets, leaving much room for invention.

In any event, the families decided to move. "When my ancestors came up here, they came right up the Connecticut (River)," Harold tells me. Which branch of the family he speaks of is unclear, and irrelevant—the river was the only effective way north, and both families eventually made the trip...and the natives who so beset his ancestors traveled upon it, too.

"In the winter time, the river froze and they walked right up," he explains. "And then they had flat boats," that could transport livestock as well as the sparing amount of clothes and sundries necessary to establish entire families in the northern wilderness. The first of the Gilletts to make their way north were Israel and John, whose father Ebenezer Gillit (the spelling evolved subtly) signed the Charter of the Town of Hartford—though Ebenezer never went there.

Benjamin Wright, Harold's great, great, great grandfather, also signed the charter, just one line away from Benjamin's; their names were destined to come closer still as the town's history unfolded.

On June 8, 1922, Helen Gillette married Seaver David Wright, with whom she bore four children. "The Gillettes and the Wrights," Harold says, "when they got married, that was the last, probably, chance of two of the original signers of the charter having any progeny." His words are at once sweet, wistful, and reverent as he talks about his parents. Harold sounds almost sad that two such bloodlines will conceivably never cross in White River Junction again—Vermonters, though not alone in this regard, are quite proud of having longstanding family ties to their state and villages. With each new generation, the one before it gets folded back into history, back among the rich complexities that weave their ties to the land. There is something deeply meaningful about understanding the history you came from—a value with profound hold on the Wright family.

Which brings us to Harold's life growing up in a home built generations before—the home in which we sit during this late winter of his seventy ninth year. "My grandfather came here (to this house) on January 10th, 1883," he says; that was the day his grandfather—Seth Wright—wed Lena Seaver. The home became the new Wright family homestead, which included then as it does now, a small second house a stone's throw up the two-lane highway that runs through their property.

Harold's brother Edward was born in that house in 1924 and lives there presently.

Harold's green eyes glisten like heirloom emeralds, his voice speeding up as he recalls his childhood. "Grandmother and grandfather used to have ham hung from the ceiling...in the cellar, where it was cool," he says, continuing "every now and then they'd say to go down and get that ham, and they'd cut off a piece. My mother would do the same thing. She'd have ham, bacon," hanging in that same cellar after she established housekeeping in that home. The meat was cooled naturally in the earthen basement, or packed away in barrels between layers of bran for longer storage. His trips to the cellar were among the many chores that came with growing up on a farm in the Green Mountains.

"We'd cut corn by hand," he says with a smile belaying his pride in the work; he seems almost eager to work those fields by hand again. Memory and nostalgia round sharp corners and tint the lighting, often shaping memories into what we want to remember rather than actual facts and conditions, but his love for the land is genuine—it shows in his smile, in the way he holds his sun-wrinkled hands. "We didn't have the fancy pickers we do today; we'd pick it by hand and throw it into a wagon," he continues. "Two people would take two rows apiece, and one person would drive the horses and a wagon. And after those two went through, a person would cut those four rows by hand. Then you'd pick four more rows, bring it down, and store it on the barn floor." It was all in a day's work, and many days' work throughout the seasons. Harold and his three brothers, Seaver David Jr., Edward, and Donald, helped the family weather the Great Depression by working this land and

126

laboring on other farms when their chores relented.

"We worked for different people, weekends, summers," he says, "and worked at home of course. We'd get a dollar a day and a meal—lunch. We used to pull kale in the cornfields by hand. It was pretty good work." While he was raised with the Christian work ethic—that work and working are good in and of themselves—as a boy he was motivated by slightly more worldly goals.

"We'd do our chores, and get done, and we'd be good so we could go to the church supper," with its wide variety of good food...and girls. As a lad he went to the Congregational Church in Hartford, before the family transferred membership to the Methodist Church in White River in the 1940s. The church suppers were quite the social affairs, where rural families and factory workers had a chance to mix—the farm and village came together over chicken pies, roast beef and Jesus.

He leans towards me, putting a hand upon the table, eyes twinkling. "If we did well," he says like a big brother making a promise he doesn't want to jinx, "they had a circus that came through town, and we could go! It used to come by train. They would have a parade in White River, and the...parade would be so long that it come up South Main, come up around North Main, and through by the Catholic Church, Church Street, and the end of it would be still coming by when the first of it got clear around!" But there was always work before play. When the strawberries were ripe in his family's patch, they would harvest them by hand and load the pickup truck. "We'd go down the street and peddle 'em door to door," in his grandparents' tradition.

"My grandfather and grandmother used to peddle butter door to door, and eggs. They would take some of their eggs and butter to a store and exchange that for things they needed...like, sugar, or something. Most of those stores had clothing too. They'd sell 'em some shoes, some boots. They didn't change much money." Those general stores were in White River Junction, a two mile walk along a winding country road from the homestead. It seemed like his family lived in a series of Gene Pelham paintings, these little snapshots of ragamuffin kids with big smiles selling strawberries so they could go to the circus...but lest we slip into kitschy nostalgia, Harold offers some stories from the tougher side of country life.

"A lot of people talk about the 'good old days,' and I think there were some good old days," he couches his transition. "But there were also some problems. They didn't have any sorts of medicines that we do today. Whole families were wiped out with diphtheria and scarlet fever, whooping cough. I've heard my grandfather talk about different families around the area here that were just gone. All dead. That wasn't one of the good old days."

Neither were the Indian attacks that plagued their family in the late 1600s, romantic as the stories might read to modern eyes. I read more quaint country idealism into Seth and Lena's door-to-door entrepreneurship than they likely felt while lugging pounds of butter and baskets of eggs into market at the general stores. Harold might sound nostalgic now about peddling strawberries and cutting corn by hand, but how did he feel at twilight so long ago, with callused palms and sunburn? Pelham's paintings are beautiful, these stories sound romantic, but black flies swarm thick in the background—little details that take the shine off, making them the first to be erased

128

or ignored.

The railroad took some of the Wrights' produce far away to Boston and Springfield and returned with big-city goods in thundering boxcars. The Connecticut River Valley was filled with family farms like the Wrights', and trading goods between the rural and village economies maintained each in a working balance of production and consumption. The farmers' surplus food fed the city folk, which freed them from agriculture to work in the mills or the thriving railroad business downtown. In turn, they provided the specialty items and money the farmers needed.

In this manner Vermont was settled with villages and towns—several of the former often comprising one of the latter, as seen in the villages within the Town of Hartford—growing first along the rivers and then along the railroads. During Harold's life, White River became the junction of Interstate 89 West from New Hampshire and I-91 North from Massachusetts. The mid-twentieth century brought to White River the junction of agricultural tradition and urbanization, and the birth of Harold Wright.

"We used to be pretty self-sufficient," Harold recalls proudly. Farmers of old were known for their thrift—particularly the Vermonters, and particularly during the Great Depression. "I never had any new clothes 'til I was probably in high school," he says, adding how, during his Depression-era childhood, very little was wasted. Most everything the family needed was available in some way through the farm. One Thanksgiving, "Everything we had for dinner was raised on the farm," he says. "The only thing my mother missed, it was a little faux pas, was she used some white sugar she'd bought. We had turkey, of course, vegetables, squash…everything, except for, she used some sugar in something, and she wished she hadn't; she had maple syrup she could have used."

That pride in independence, in taking care of themselves, is common among the Vermonters I know—those of Harold's generation, and younger. There is something in the rustic mountains, the smell of pine trees in springtime and the feel of dirt under the fingernails that draws them from bed in the morning and comforts them on the farm, in the factories, or wherever they find employment. The railroads running through White River Junction to New York, Canada, and Boston were all laid by hand. Steam engines carried boxcars full of produce from the farms, textiles and paper from the mills, animal hides from the tanneries and lumber from the hills, produced for generations by the hands of Vermonters. Harold remembers harvesting crops by hand before the family could afford cultivators, and felling timber with a jagged-tooth team saw.

Carrying that saw with naïve teenage confidence, Harold and his older brother Edward set forth to fell the biggest tree on their side of the mountains. "It must have been about 1940," he says, making him roughly fourteen years old at the time. "We told our father and mother that we were going to cut that tree, and they said 'well be careful,' and away we went! We had a six-foot crosscut saw, and it was so big, we got halfway through, and we could only move it a little bit! We had to take it out a couple times and clean the sawdust out. My father came over when we were probably halfway through it, and he waited until we got it cut down. It was so big, we didn't know if we could draw it with our horses!" They cut it into twelve foot sections, these two boys who couldn't be stopped by the biggest tree on the mountain.

World War II darkened his high school days, a terrifying cloud on the horizon for most of America's young men. At seventeen he enlisted in the Army under the agreement that he could graduate high school before they took him. He did, they did, and he found himself "sent up to Virginia, to a map reproduction school." The boy from Vermont "would go out in the morning and take pictures of everything. Then we'd develop those pictures, and enlarge them, and the instructor, who was excellent, he would pinpoint one part and say 'this, I want you to blow it up,' and we'd have to go back and blow that area up and point out all the little things." Their definition of "blow up" was of course to enlarge, rather than explode, aerial and scout photographs.

After bombing runs the Allies photographed the damage to assess the enemy's remaining strength. Harold was supposed to develop those photographs in Europe, but "by the time I was ready to go, they'd finished the European theatre. That was ended, and we got all kinds of shots for this and that and the other for Japan." Then in the morning of August 15, 1945, he helped the base newspaper print the V-J Day Special Edition.

"They gave us a chance to enlist for three years in the Army of Occupation, or go home," he recalls. "I thought 'I'll get out of this thing as fast as I can,'" so he went home to Vermont rather than deploy to Europe as a peacekeeper. Now sixty years after he chose that early, honorable discharge, there are "two things I would do over," in life: pursue a college education, and sign up to go to Europe after all—but not for heroic reasons.

"Some of these fellars went," he says, "and they had

131

a three year vacation in Europe! They went to Germany of course, but they went to Italy, France, Switzerland... They would be with the Army, they had restrictions, but there was no fighting. They had very liberal time off... How much would it cost you to do that as a civilian?"

Home drew him back from Virginia, though, up the rails along the same river his ancestors traced. He worked on the farm again, but found that rural life as he had known it was rapidly changing.

White River Junction had long relied upon the Cone Paper Mill and the International Paper Mill, the railroads, and the farmers in a complicated balance of supply, demand, and employment. But the railways saw less commerce after the war, as more highways were cleared through the mountains. Big mills scaled back their manpower, or shut down, such as the Harris-Emery Company in the nearby Queechee Village that closed in February of 1951.

The Ward Baking Company, like other businesses, automated much of their production and drastically reduced their manpower after the war. Family farms gave way to a new phenomenon: the large-scale business farm, where dairy cattle had numbers instead of names and fields stretched well beyond what any family could pick by hand. Farmers sold their land by degrees or wholesale lots, many turning to city jobs or the employ of conglomerate farms. While many family farms operate to this day upon more or less the same land, crops, and types of cattle as they have for generations, this was an unprecedented paradigm shift in Harold's "Greatest Generation."

Change came to Harold's personal life in 1950, too: on June 24th he married his sweetheart Maxine Harford.

Nine months and two days later they welcomed the first of the next generation of Wrights, daughter Gail. Grandpa Seaver Wright saw the births of his grandchildren Harold, Richard, and Bruce, before passing away on December 4th, 1956; the old farmer did not live to see Harold get a city job.

"The farm wasn't big enough to support myself and the family, everyone here," Harold explains, "so we had to have additional (income from) outside the farm." Some of that income came from hard labor at the rail yard unloading hundred-pound bags of government-supplied fertilizer. "The government used to buy super phosphate for the farmers," he says. "They had to hire somebody to unload it from the freight cars, and I got fifty cents a ton. If you had a twenty ton car, you got ten dollars for unloading the fertilizer. It took all day, and boy that was really making money! If you were really lucky, you could get two cars at the same time, forty tons!" Twenty bucks!

Harold sits back in his wooden chair, lost in a memory. "I remember one time, this guy came. He had a dump truck with a very short wheelbase, and he wasn't too overly ambitious. He had two tons. We were unloading it into his truck, and he said 'put it on the back end, 'cause I gotta unload this stuff, and I don't want to lug it.' So we put it right on the back end of his truck, and he was backed right up square to the cargo door. He signed his paperwork and drove away, and of course with all the weight on the back end, his truck went right up in the air! It dumped it all right on the ground!" He laughs a kind-hearted chuckle as his story fades into the walls.

Like working on the farm, in this job he was his own

boss and worked with his hands. Also like on the farm, his work helped other people. Perhaps he complained back then, about the hours or backaches, but not as he talked to me. His next railroad anecdote, though I risk wearing them thin, shows me more about his integrity— and how he balances it with common sense.

"One year I got a notice from some administrator," he says. "He wanted me to weigh ten bags. So I took the bags down and weighed them, hundred pounds, hundred pounds, hundred pounds...the guys in the freight house were laughing at me! 'What are you doin' that for,' they said, 'the other guy never did that!' Well I don't know. I got a letter sayin' I was supposed to, and threatened me with all kinds of problems if I didn't do it, so I weighed them all and put them back in the car. Every bag weighed a hundred pounds. I get this nasty letter back from the guy saying 'next time I want you to weigh 'em, not just write down a hundred pounds!' 'Cause apparently sometimes they weigh 98, or 102, but that was the last time I weighed 'em! The next time, I wrote down 101, 99, and I never heard back from him!"

Ever vigilant for opportunity, Harold took a long, hopeful look at what was then the US Postal Department. His father Seaver had been a substitute rural mail carrier, as well as a Justice of the Peace. The latter was familiar to the Wright family, as his grandfather Seth Wright had been a Justice of the Peace around the turn of the twentieth century. The tradition continued when Seaver resigned, shortly before his death, and Harold succeeded him. The son took his father's roles to the next level, though, taking a Post Office job full time. The homestead remained in operation as a dairy farm, growing vegetables and producing milk for sale and

134

personal use. They had chickens, and maintained a sty under the barn for pigs. Timber came as needed from the forests covering their side of the mountain. They were making a go of their agricultural heritage, but life and traditions were changing all around.

* * * * *

The smell of Maxine's cookies is amazing, and we both fall silent as she serves us a pot of strong coffee and a plate mounded over. Outside some stray snow flurries cling to the frozen, abnormally snowless ground, a pleasantly cold scene to watch with hot coffee in my hand. I bite into my first cookie as a logging truck rumbles past on the highway a few yards from the porch.

It tastes wonderful—the cookie, not the truck—and I thank Maxine for her kindness. Harold gets distracted watching a man walking along the road. The man, he says, lives in the Wrights' smaller house, a few yards nearer town and in plain sight through the dining room window. "I wonder what he…" Harold trails off, speculating a moment later, "the mail's already come through. Well maybe he just…I don't know."

"Who is that?" I ask naïvely.

"That's Edward, my brother!"

"Oh."

Harold swirls a little sugar into his coffee. "He's two years older, he's eighty one. He was born in that house, and I think he plans to die in it. My mother wanted one pure Vermonter, so when Edward was born, he was born at home. In those days they had home deliveries." He pauses, then the old postman adds "1412 North Hartland. He's an old bat." Harold was born in the hospital in Lebanon, New Hampshire, just across the Connecticut River; but his brother, he asserts, is a full-fledged Vermonter. This concept of a "pure Vermonter" intrigues me, as I have seen it in several other Vermonters I know, and have encountered the phenomenon of pride in being a "pure" something-or-other in older Americans from other states as well—it seems a widespread phenomenon, specific here in the state's name alone.

My friends explained that a "pure Vermonter" is raised in the state, of course, but has to be born there as well—with bonus points if they are born at home. If that act, birth and all that comes with it, happens across state lines…well, that's a demerit that even a lifetime of living on the homestead and working the land by hand can't undo.

While home deliveries were the way of the world before modern medicine, hospitals were readily available in the 1920s—like the one where Harold was born just two years after his brother was born at home. Their mother's desire to have a "true Vermonter" has far less to do with medicine and convenience, and much more to do with valuing their ties to the land—ties they wanted, as many still want today, to forge for their children from the very moment of birth.

As I mull this over, Harold asks "where was I?"

"Mail carrier," I sputter through a mouthful of cookies.

"Right. We had one old lady that's sister lived farther on the route. They were twins, in fact. She used to leave a bag for her sister, and put out a note for the Postmaster, 'please leave this with so-and-so farther out the route.' We were supposed to charge postage, but we never did."

Those were the days Norman Rockwell painted, when the mailman knew almost everyone on his route; when the simple address "Joe Pogar, Wilder, Vermont," was all you needed to get a letter through.

The mail was a steady link to the outside world for rural Vermonters before television; before telephones, even. It brought milk checks to dairy farmers, word from far-flung siblings or elderly parents, mail order catalogues that brought the world to their doors... And sometimes the mailman would come right to your door himself, dropping off a package that was too big for the mailbox or hand-delivering an important parcel.

"You found out all the gossip," Harold remembers with a grin. "Who was not staying home nights, who was on the road, who was going to have a baby... The mailman was quite important for communication! A lot of people looked forward to that, it was their tie to the outside world.

"And boy, if you didn't have the milk checks for some people, you'd better just go right by! Some of 'em would be right out there. If you didn't have something that they were lookin' for that you should have, they would look in your vehicle, and say 'I know you've got it in here somewhere!' Boy, they'd get real upset about that, but if you didn't have it, you didn't have it!"

That was back when they knew everyone on their route, and their dogs as well—before postmen carried dog mace, because they could subdue a pooch by calling its name. But what if he were to leave this afternoon, head out into the cold and walk the old routes again... would he still recognize the names on the mailboxes and know who to find behind which door?

"No," he says in a heavy tone. The sense of community

White River Junction—and many small towns across America—enjoyed for generations has seen great decline in Harold's life. His eyes show a tinge of regret, a private lament as he carefully chooses his words. "The town's changed traumatically. Down at the south end were the old Italian families, some of which came over straight from Italy, and they were large families." He does not explain why he says traumatically rather than dramatically, and I immediately regret not asking as he carries on, "many of them came for the railroads. That was sort of their section of town. Up on the terraces, there were more, well, bankers, bakers, people that maybe were a little better off.

"Over on the other side of the river," he continues, "there was more of the blue collar type worker; they were working in the plants." Jobs used to be plentiful in the villages, and in all sorts of vocations. "In White River, George West had quite a big bakery there. They worked 'round the clock, and their bread trucks went all over the state. Quite a few of those people lived right there, and on the terraces behind. I don't think, probably ten percent of the people are still in their homes. Some of the people are the next generation, some, the third generation. Quite a turnover."

1958 saw Herald trade his mailbag for a desk when the White River Junction Postmaster retired. "I took that job," he explains very carefully, "'cause I think I told you earlier on, I tried to earn money to supplement the farm here any way I could." There was more to the job than just being a manager, and there was more to applying than just showing up. "You had to take the Civil Service Exam," he recalls. "I was a five-point veteran, and I got a ninety-three on the exam,
138

and with that I got a ninety-eight." His name and score were forwarded to Senator George Akin, along with Harold's registered political affiliation—Republican—filed earlier as a compulsory part of being a Justice of the Peace. His application went all the way to President Eisenhower. "A Postmaster in those days was the same as an ambassador," he remembers. "Your name had to be submitted from the President and confirmed by the Senate. I was appointed officially August 22nd, 1958, as Postmaster for White River Junction."

He worked in the sturdy granite and brick Post Office along South Main Street, managing fourteen employees. It was built "in '34, I think it was," he says. "That was built right, from the old plans. If they wanted a bomb shelter, they could go down there. We were probably the safest building in the whole area!"

To say that he ran his office like a tight ship might be a bit dramatic, but not without some grounds: "The Postmaster was in the same (legal) category as the captain of a ship," Harold explains with whimsy. Although his ancestors had been attacked by Indians, to my knowledge his Post Office was never beset by pirates.

Their building faced directly onto a rail siding where Central Vermont and Boston & Maine cars pulled past daily. They sent the area's southbound mail to Boston in a car with a few clerks who rode the train sorting envelopes and packages. Everything was in order by the time they reached Boston, where they would pick up a northbound load and sort it on their way back. Though the railroad traffic diminished, the mail increased. The highways and agricultural revolution enabled more people to live conveniently in the Green Mountain State.

As the mail service increased, so did Harold's staff.

Truck shipments replaced train deliveries as the rails fell ever quieter. The staff grew, and Harold realized he had a propitious problem: the little White River Junction Post Office was inundated with mail, and rapidly growing into a branch responsible for routing mail throughout the Vermont side of the Connecticut River Valley. They needed a larger facility, and Harold was among the leaders who set forth to build one.

"You talk about building a building quick!" he laughs, shaking his head. "The day before July there were four of us who stood near (where) the bus terminal is. O'Conner from the Postal Inspection Service, Frank Gilman, Dayton Wakefield and myself met and he wanted a sixty foot by one-hundred-seventy foot, one-story building with thirteen doors, docks where trucks could back up to, and when do you think they wanted it done?" He looks me hard in the eye, like a stern foreman. I have no idea.

"This was July, and they wanted it done by August 20th!" he blurts, laughing. "Frank Gilman said 'yeah, I think I can do it.' That same day he was out there with his bulldozer digging temporary fittings!" Now his eyes soften as the corners of his mouth draw higher, smiling and shaking his head ever so slightly. "On August 20th we moved in. The trucks started coming in from all over. Burlington, Boston, Springfield...we used that for maybe four, five years." He orchestrated the land purchase and construction for the current facility on Sykes Avenue, which Harold dedicated on October 18th, 1964, and which operates to this day.

Living on the farm, working in the city, he experienced a bit of two different lifestyles. "It was the best of two worlds," he says, "because I was able to come home to dinner every day. Ten minutes to come home," a short drive or pleasant walk in good weather. His mornings would start before sunrise with the morning milking, and not end until after sunset and the evening milking. The farm responsibilities did not diminish—the village job just crowded them out, pushing them earlier or later in the day. Sometimes they started at three o'clock when machinery needed fixing before the morning routine; occasionally Harold Jr. had to come home from his job in town to take care of something. Though the Wrights managed, there were challenges in balancing their city and country lives.

The Wright family farm continued as a commercial dairy farm, the milking machines running twice daily to relieve their fifty-some-odd cows. "We were one of the biggest herds in the DHI (Dairy Herd Improvement) Association," Harold says in such a way that does not sound like bragging. Though no longer the primary source of family income, the farm provided necessary food and funds; Harold and Maxine were blessed with six children and the continued health of his elderly mother, Helen. They lived together as the second, third, and fourth generations of Wrights occupying the homestead. As there are few connections to homes and land stronger than birth and death, there are few connections to White River Junction stronger than those of the seven generations (and counting) of the Wright family in the area—ties made sadly stronger with the passing of Bruce David Wright in the fields behind the homestead on October 10th, 1971.

"Bruce was probably one of the safest of our children," his father recalls with a strong voice. "He had taken all the safety driving things at school. He was very safety conscious. That morning he took the tractor, it was during bow and arrow season. He went up to find Richard, his older brother. He tipped the tractor on a bank, and it killed him instantly. He was buried up here in Hartford. Many of our ancestors are buried up there in the Hartford Cemetery, and quite a few in the Wilder Cemetery, the relatives of my mother's. There's many things that have happened over the years since we got married here," he says, trailing off. Old pain blends with pride, joy and sorrow balanced like the seasons. They come together in his smile, a smile that mixes nostalgia with hope. After a moment's respectful silence, I ask more about his job as Postmaster.

Aside from administration and expanding the Post Office, Harold walked the routes once a year. "We found out where carriers were hiding on light days," he says mischievously. Then he turns ever-so-slightly more serious. "My main thing was to the carriers, if you have a light day, don't hang out at the Legion, or the Polka Dot restaurant; if you're going to beat your schedule, stop in at John Doe's and visit with them a few minutes, keep out of sight." The postman had to stay abreast the local gossip, after all, even as the routes grew longer and strangers moved into the community; but he needn't become part of it by slouching in public.

An opportunity came up for Harold to work at a Post Office in Boston, so he checked it out. The decision was simple: thanks, but no. "I went down for a week, and, well, you just were an individual in a sea of people and you didn't know anybody," he says dismally. "Dean Davis, he was a governor here, and he said 'we've got air in Vermont that's never been breathed.' Now you go down to New York, Philadelphia, Boston, they don't have any air that's never been breathed!" We look out of the picture window in unison, towards the rolling fields and distant mountains. Everything in sight belongs to his family: his son Richard's sawmill across the road, his brother Edward's home, the fields, the trees, and years of stories, blood, and laughter folded neatly into the soil. He does not speak ill of Boston—he does not speak ill without necessity—but this is clearly home.

His parents, grandparents, and family back through the centuries and across New England were born to farmers, and to be farmers. For many of them, that meant living, working, and dying at the homestead just outside of White River Junction. There was little choice in the matter for most of them; but then there was Helen Wright, Harold's grandmother. She graduated from Smith College, a remarkable accomplishment for a woman in the 1800s, and crossed that cultural divide between rural and city life to become a teacher. Seth Wright was a Town Lister and Justice of the Peace, the latter claimed in turn by Seaver Wright. But not until Harold did a family member spend such a long career in city work. Indeed, it was with one shoe polished and another tracking mud that he opened his family to careers beyond agriculture.

Harold's grandmother instilled in him a deep respect for education, and he came to regret not getting a college education after returning from the service. When his son Richard had an opportunity to go to college on a football scholarship, Harold encouraged his son as best he could. They flew around the country together, looking for a college with the right balance of sports and education. Though he received a football scholarship to the University of Vermont, Richard needed better grades to be accepted as a student; he attended Bridgeton, Maine to boost his grades, but a shoulder injury playing for Bridgeton against Norwich ended Richard's days playing football...and his hopes of riding a sports scholarship. He soon left school and returned to White River Junction.

While their roots are in the family farm, and their houses are surrounded by fields, Richard is presently the only Wright who is truly living off the land. Fifty two years old today, and a father, Richard operates the sawmill across the road. With saws, grinders, tractors, a kiln, and other equipment, he renders trees from his family's land into finished lumber, and lives on ten acres "out back" in a home he built.

Education took hold in his sisters Donna and Anne, leading them to careers in teaching. "Donna is our youngest daughter," Harold explains. "She works here in White River. She works with special needs people, I guess you call someone that could be a problem in class. Anne is our next daughter, she teaches kindergarten," and has for twenty-three years. "Bruce, the one who got killed, was next, then Richard, the one who runs the sawmill. He got into lumber and I don't know where he's going to stop. Then Harold, our next boy, he's at Gateway. He's been there thirty years; he's in the parts department. Then Gail, our oldest daughter, she has a catering business. She has a deal with Signal, the airport where the jets come in. She has a deal for the pilots..."

They worked on the family farm as children, and still help where they are needed, but their professional lives have taken them out of the cornrows and into classrooms, kitchens, and warehouses. Harold spanned the divide between the classic Vermont agrarian tradition and the ever-expanding city, his example forming a bridge his children walked across to new careers.

Harold served White River Junction through the close of his thirtieth year as Postmaster. On August 22nd, 1988, at the age of sixty-two, he retired with full honors and a warm send off. He received a clock bearing a commemorative plaque inscribed "Harold B. Wright MSC Manager USPS, White River Junction, VT 05001, 8-22-58 thru 8-22-88." He gave them thirty years' service and a forty-thousand square foot regional branch, and they gave him a clock. As a modest man, it was, perhaps even at that, an unnecessary token. Though displayed on the dining room wall, it's not working today, and I have to stare at it for awhile before he explains its significance. Harold is a proud Vermonter, but a modest man.

Three years shy of the national retirement age back then, Harold felt retirement was the right move at the right time in his life—there was so much more he wanted to see. "I wanted to do some things outside," he explains. "You know, if you have a job like that, you're pretty tied up." Mainly he wanted to see, and show Maxine, the world beyond White River Junction while they could still enjoy the travel. They flew to Jersey, in the Channel Islands between England and France, with the American Jersey Cattle Club.

"Jerseys originated on the Channel Islands, on Jersey," he explains. They saw more than cows, though. "If you ever want a little trivia question, ask how many places the Germans occupied in the United Kingdom."

The Nazis occupied part of the United Kingdom? I wondered.

"The UK didn't defend the island," he says, reveling in his role as history teacher, "and some of the people were upset that the English didn't defend it. But it was not a strategic point." The Germans invaded the islands with little difficulty, but then they had to manage an agrarian society as proud of their land—and as fiercely independent—as any Vermonter. Harold and Maxine visited farms and homes and spoke with dairymen about their common interests, and the peculiar history of Jersey. The more they visited, the better they got along with the English; through their stories, Harold and Maxine could relate to these Englishmen.

"They (the Nazis) built a huge underground hospital, scary as the devil," he recalls from under a heavy brow; his face is hard now, as if stuck fast between fear and awe. "They had operating suites in there, they had telephone communications, you go in there and it'd scare you. That was the closest place to England, and they wanted this as a place they could drop off injured troops quickly. I went once, but the second time I went back, I didn't go back, I didn't need that," he says with absolution, as if to say he has no desire to visit the grim side of the conflict he narrowly avoided. He is very glad to have missed the war, even if he regrets not seeing Europe for free as a peacekeeper.

"The German occupants came to the head of the island people," he says, switching to a lighter story, "and the Germans said to the High Bailiff, 'you keep your people under control and I'll take care of my soldiers. We don't want them to abuse you, but we want you to do as you're told.' And one of the first things they did was turn in all of their radios, and all of their guns. But a few hung onto their radios, and a few hung onto their guns." This information came from a friend they made—the daughter of that High Bailiff.

Her father kept his guns and his radio, defiantly tuning in to the BBC every evening for news about the war, exactly as I imagine Harold would if, somehow, Vermont was ever captured by a foreign army. "He had his radio hid in his chimney," Harold says with glee, "behind some bricks! He'd pull out, take his radio out, and put on his headset and he'd get the BBC news from London. Within a few minutes, he'd put it back, seal it all up, put a picture or two around it, and he'd spread the word around 'the English bombed such and such a place today...' They kept the island people informed of what's going on."

Sounds like something a Vermonter would do...

"How familiar did it look," I ask, searching for more about his connection to Jersey, "from what you've been seeing and doing your whole life? You made friends, but how did you relate with the people?"

"I think they are quite similar," he says, pausing a moment, tilting his head just a bit. "I was impressed by the farms I saw in England, they were huge, huge fields. Now Jersey and Guernsey, they're both in the Gulf Stream, they're probably planting their crops now (in late autumn). They plant potatoes early, in February, and they have the earliest potatoes to ship to the UK." Typically those potatoes reach the market before the French crop just a hop south—a point of considerable English pride. It delights Harold, who wears a victor's smile as if it was his own crop—as if he shares a connection with those farmers strong enough to share also in their triumph.

Rather than expound on that, which is not the sort

of thing a Vermonter would do anyway, Harold tells me more about the underground hospital—about the slave labor they used and how the sick and the slow would be dumped into the concrete as examples to the rest. He speaks of the disappearing coastline on Jersey, nearly a mile of which is exposed at low tide and awash when the waves come back in, and how some farmers harvest seaweed there to dry and burn for fuel or use as fertilizer. He tells me such interesting things about the people and their history, and then sums it all up—visits he made, their wartime resistance, the Jersey cows and potatoes—with a simple recommendation: "Jersey, if you ever get a chance, you need to check it out."

He and Maxine also visited an embarkation point for Allied troops invading occupied France, and sites in France where he could have been stationed during the war. The lingering effects of his abbreviated military service are hard to trace, but are there nonetheless.

First scheduled for Europe, he was later scheduled to serve in the Pacific, and received all of the preparatory immunizations…just before V-J Day. Does he have the same regret about not seeing the Far East as not touring Europe? "I just have no interest in Japan," he says, shaking his head as if the idea is actually repugnant. "If someone said today that they had a free trip to Japan (for me), I don't think I'd go. I don't care for that, but some do."

I tell him that I do, and that I have travelled many times to Asia; he seems neither surprised nor impressed, nor even interested. In dismissing the Far East, he did not slander it. This is a trait I respect in Harold, and folks of his generation; it is a trait I do not often encounter in those my own age, who too frequently disparage

Dave Norman

that which they are simply uninterested in as means of further distancing themselves. Perhaps Harold's tact is peculiar to his generation. Perhaps it is something my peers will acquire later in life. At any rate, his offense-less way of dismissing the things that do not interest him reminds me of other Vermonters I've met—indeed, of good country folks from across New England.

A few years ago he toured the Canadian Rockies with the same group that brought him to Jersey. They went to the Stampede in Calgary, a huge rodeo where top prize finishers win big money and second place earns a ribbon. "Those are real cowboys there!" he says with a wide smile of admiration—and a hint of jealousy. A trip south took their group to farms and ranches in Texas, and for a few hours to Mexico. "I bought a belt, and we had lunch," he recalls of their jaunt across the border; that is all he says about Mexico, and at that, without any particular emotion or interest. Though he likes traveling to see other rural areas, he says he is always happy to come home. He loves this land, his family homestead, and passed up an offer in the '80s to sell it for a staggering three million dollars; today he quietly sips coffee with me in his grandfather's dining room.

The were fifty-some cows on his dairy farm at the dawn of the twenty first century, but his was no longer one of the largest herds in the DHI—the era of the family farm passed while Harold was at work in town.

Those family farms that remain either scrape by, supplement their income as Harold did with other jobs, or have turned to "organic" farming, where the cattle are given untreated food and never receive hormones. Operating costs are high and certifications are a hassle, but organic farmers can command higher prices for their milk, meat, and produce, and thus earn enough to live.

Harold's farm kept going as it had for generations, while other small farms either changed with the times or sold out to corporations. "I was just reading today," Harold says, "that somewhere in New Mexico they just opened up an area, and they're not going to milk less than 2,000 cows. There are places up in Wisconsin that want to do business with just a few people, not (just) everybody." His voice belies a sense of awe, and I try to imagine two-thousand head of cattle roaming Harold's land; it is hard for either of us to picture, and neither of us wants a thing to do with milking 2,000 cows twice a day.

Though operating costs increased, the return for the family farmer remained similar; with inflation, it bought less.

There is still plenty to be done on five-hundred acres without a full dairy operation or large crops— especially for a family man nearing his eighties. When Harold considered phasing out the dairy and wide scale planting, Richard was just getting into timber cutting with his mill; none of the other Wright children had any professional stake in the land. They sold off the cows and on April 4th, 2004, the Wright family farm ceased traditional operations. "That was four, four, oh-four," he says by way of explanation, though he says nothing of the significance beyond the quirk with the numbers.

Their homestead is now more of a recreational farm, if such a thing truly exists. The man born into agriculture, who stepped so confidently into city work, retired to close his farm. His homestead is surrounded by the family's land, but the old business is interred in
150

paperwork, the envelopes marked "—4.4.04."

"When you go back today," he says, setting his empty coffee cup down on a small saucer, "you might stop and see that tomb there." It would cap my interview with Harold by paying my respects to his forebears. "It's just about a mile plus up there, past Wright Reservoir Road, just after you go under the interstate. Instead of turning and squeaking around right towards the motel, just go straight and it'll be right there on your left in front of Allen Pools, or just before you get to the Carriage Shed." I know where he means; but the Wright Reservoir— there must a connection.

"They had three, I think it is," he explains, "or four, right around here. Reservoirs were the supplies of water for the towns and villages. When they originally chartered the town, they had to provide some land for churches, schools, and I think reservoirs came in there somewhere."

Benjamin Wright, having received a large land grant from the Crown in England, donated a pond on his land for the town—the Wright Reservoir. "There were at least four reservoirs right nearby here. There's one just up the road here," Harold says; he does not draw the explicit connection. Does he figure it's just that obvious—one of those facts about ourselves and our histories that makes too much sense to explain? The holes we leave in our stories tell as much as the details we include, for they show states of mind; they bespeak a familiarity that cannot be shown so well any other way, and help us make the stories relevant to our own lives and circumstances.

But they open small doors for big problems; filling in the gaps ourselves practically invites misunderstanding and disaster. Maybe someone else with the same last name donated the reservoir, and in my assumption, I miss a fantastic story. It's not likely (nor is it the case), but possible. When we fill in those lapses in our research or memory or someone else's story—when a writer weaves the facts into a larger framework—we risk getting things wrong and changing the very meaning of the narrative.

Such tiny holes, inviting such innocent assumptions, account for so much of the friction between writer and source—between a storyteller and someone who was there. There has been no friction here, yet, though I am aware of the risk. Perhaps that framework I add to his stories, to hold them all together and make them more meaningful than just telling one man's specific life, gets it all wrong; if not wrong, then different, and is that not a shade of the same color?

Consider, though, that the way each new generation fills in the gaps and frames the stories keeps them alive—and current. Updated. Relevant... What is it about the struggles of a generation well before our time, or of people we will never meet, that makes them interesting? In part it could be the way they're told—as if they could be our own. The tenor might change; a fact might change; but in these little spaces every narrator leaves, we find finger holds to get our own grip on the story.

But in this daydream I digress; this is, after all, Harold's story, and he is telling me something about the reservoirs...

"Quite a few years ago they decided that that water wasn't fit to drink, so they put in a few wells," he continues, his words coming ever-so-slightly faster as he leans forward a bit in his chair. "If people knew anything, they would have seen why it wasn't fit to drink. There was a Frenchman and his wife logging up in there. This guy had a shanty, a pair of horses. You know where they put the manure? He put the shanty right by the brook, so all he had to do was open the door and it was gone!" Life was different before zoning laws, yes, that's obvious…but there he gives a fabulous example of how, and by entertaining me, conceals the dry fact in a funny story.

"We had another pair of brothers," he says, "they were logging over the other way. They were French. They came from Claremont, and had a little tractor, a John Deere tractor, and a horse. They knew what they were doin', and could fell a tree just where you want it. They were logging down here for us, and they got done cuttin'. So they moved. They had an old Ford truck, with just a set of logging bungs on it. They put the horse in the shanty, backed the truck up to where the shanty was, took the tractor, and pushed the horse, and the shanty, onto the truck. They went up by here with the horse sticking its head out the door of the shanty on the truck, and they were going up to Wilder.

"I said 'now how are you going to get that horse and shanty off the truck?' 'Cause the tractor was up here where they pushed it on. They said 'oh, no trouble, no trouble! We'll back up to a big tree, put the chain around the big tree, and have it hitched to the tree, then drive away. Out come shanty, out come horse, come back and get tractor.' They went back down by awhile later, with no shanty, and no horse, and went back by a little while later with the tractor on the truck!" His stories are pretty cool; they might not mean anything—then again, they might—but I like them, and sometimes just liking a thing is good enough. I ask about other local color, and he smiles—it's nice to have someone who listens, and I'm happy to oblige.

"They built a boat in the cellar of one guy's house," he continues, clasping his hands on his lap. "They built the boat too big (and) couldn't get the boat out of the cellar! I asked 'how'd you get your boat out?' 'Oh, no problem! We break bulkhead!' To get the boat out to go fishing!" We chuckle our way into a comfortable silence. Harold shifts a bit in his chair, looks at his watch, out the window, and then back to me.

* * * * *

The interview has come full circle, from the Wrights' early days in Vermont through a recent trip to Europe, and back again to a pair of French lumberjacks in the old White River Junction. The cookies are gone, and Harold has work to do helping Richard over at the sawmill. There is energy, surprising energy, in Harold's eyes—the energy to get outside in the cold and put in a good day's work before night falls. I am from the information generation, with a computer and an electric space heater in a nice, warm apartment; he has a tractor out in this freezing afternoon. Something about that seems backwards, but we each need to set about our work.

I thank Maxine for her hospitality, and she gives me a bag of cookies "for the road." Harold sees me off and waves goodbye as I drive towards White River Junction, following his directions to an earthen mound, parking in front of the spa store and walking to a half-acre of land sloped over the hand-laid rock tomb. The entrance bears the names of David, David Jr., Bela, Hannah, Elizabeth, and Betsy Wright with dates of death from 1814 (Hannah) to 1846 (Betsy). There's another story here—one that says a lot about David Wright's era.

"Major Wright had a great fear of being buried alive," wrote John St. Croix in <u>Historical Highlights of the Town of Hartford Vermont</u>, "and, before his death, left instructions that the cover of his coffin should not be nailed down nor the door of the tomb sealed. It is said that he had stone shelves put, one above the other, around the sides of the tomb except on the left of the entrance where he had only a lower shelf. This is where he directed his own coffin to be set and a mallet placed with him."

The great diseases back then were scarlet fever and whooping cough, and a "sleeping sickness" where the afflicted fell into a coma and took on the outward appearance of death. Without ambulances and well trained doctors standing by, most pronouncements of death were left to the head of the household...which could end badly.

A friend of mine, alive and well in our modern era, had whooping cough. He recovered from it quickly, and all the while we laughed at its funny name and the sounds he made because we do not know anyone who has ever died of whooping cough; we don't know anyone who has ever had scarlet fever, either, which seals it in the realm of inaccessible history—a fact with no feeling. I can't relate to Major Wright's fear of sleeping sickness; I can relate, though, to the horror of being buried alive. That's what keeps Poe's story "The Premature Burial" relevant; that's the connection that brings me in touch with Major Wright's lifetime, the feeling that helps me relate to the fact. Harold's words come back to me: *That wasn't one of the good old days.*

While I can't relate to Indian attacks, the stories about the Gillett family help me see a very different New England from the one in which I live. Hearing those stories, especially from Harold, makes historical anecdotes come alive so much more than simply reading names and dates—this is precisely what I need more of to understand the living history of White River Junction. I need more people; real Vermonters! Real hands to shake and real lives tied to the land, perhaps those that were at some time untied from it; real lives wrapped in historical context that makes their stories accessible to people who shared an experience no matter where or when they live. This is why I walked through the buildings, talked to Chris McKinley, ran my fingers over the nicks in the brick…to make the stories come alive.

Harold's stories are timeless—of facing great risk to improve a family's safety and prosperity (David Wright), growing up hard and fast in dangerous times while longing for the sanctity of home (John Gillett), defying norms to chase dreams and live up to one's potential (Helen Wright)…these character types, these story lines, are universal. This is what I came to find, and I found it in speaking with a local; I am lucky to realize this now, here, pacing around the tomb, while I have the time and energy to do something about it—to find more people I may learn from.

Storytelling is the oldest form of record; it is still the most prevalent for a reason. Good storytellers put meaning in traditions, names with dates and faces on names—they speak for history. The locals imbue White River Junction's story with very personal, accessible details, and might just teach me a thing or two...about my life, as well as theirs. Our greatest natural resource is the wealth of human experience available if we just take time to listen...and I know a few more Vermonters who will take time to talk.

North Main St.—Larry Chase declined to be photographed. In lieu of a picture of Larry, this is a view southeast along North Main St., showing clockwise from top center: West Lebanon homes across the Connecticut River, the Gates Block, North Main St. itself, the charred pit where the White River Amusement Pub stood before burning down several months before this photo, the Polka Dot Diner at the nine o'clock position, and the 494 locomotive on display at White River Station at center.

Larry Chase
A Big Frog in a Small Puddle

The boy stands on the concrete parade ground at Fort Devon, Vermont, one of many in rank and file and olive drab under the summer sun. A young lieutenant fresh from West Point runs them through close order drill, *guide, right!* their hands swinging just so far, toes coming just so high, *to the left, march!* and faces, stony. They ran two miles this morning, and close order drill comes just before lunch when the shadows are short and young throats are eager for water. The officer marches them to the edge of the parade ground, where another lieutenant stands in the shade of a large maple tree.

On his order the cadets break rank and take refuge in the shade, drinking from tin canteens and wiping sweat from their lips. Larry Chase looks up from the leather boots and pleated pants, up the formal dress coat past several ribbons to the stony face of a man who seems so wise—an officer of the United States Army, a representative of something larger than all of them, a man of adventure and action and other things boys idolize. Without firing a shot, without saving a soul, this man is Larry's hero—all the more for simple comforts, like seeing him while seated at last in the comforting shade. This is the summer of 1929, and Larry is thirteen years old. Now their lesson begins, today's focus on the structure of the legislative branch of the United States

Government and the checks and balances that make democracy work…and make it better than the fascism they just defeated in Europe during World War I.

Larry listens intently, curious about the country beyond his native Massachusetts, cued upon every word this hero speaks. He shakes his shoulders loose and puts down the canteen, growing comfortable in the shade, growing comfortable with these lessons. The officers extol their virtues of duty, honor, and country, and spend hours each summer explaining to cadets just what that "country" is, why it was made so, and how it works. These are good lessons that affect Larry in profound ways, though at the time it only feels like another day in the Citizen's Military Training Corps (CMTC), a special summer camp for boys who can't afford traditional camps.

That boy grew into the man sitting across a desk from me in this Hartford, Vermont home—at the other end of a life long defined by service and diligent work. Above his head hangs a shadowbox with military service and qualification medals, upon a shelf is a picture of his daughter with President George W. Bush, and somewhere in his basement is a picture of Larry Chase with the senior President Bush. Larry has called this area home for more than sixty years, and now, just past his ninetieth birthday, his identity is inextricably interwoven with the town of Hartford—specifically the village of White River Junction. Though born in Woburn, Massachusetts and raised out of state, in many ways Larry has become a Vermonter; this is the story of how that happened.

* * * * *

We speak in the office in his home, the afternoon sun streaming in upon me and warming the room like a greenhouse on this otherwise cold winter day. The floor is polished wood, the bookshelves match, and this functional office is pleasantly charming; I feel comfortable, and rest easily in my chair. Larry's bearing, even sitting at his desk, is one of pride and dignity from his leather shoes up to the shoulders he holds square and level. When he speaks, his voice is powerful but not fierce, his words solid with the weight of conviction but not cold with steely absolution. This sort of confidence is familiar from Harold Wright's voice. He asked me, when we first sat down, "what do you want to know?" Though this is my interview, following my questions, I wonder who is really in control.

There are no holidays named for him, no monuments, and that suits his humility. His legacy is in the unified school district and a central fire protection service, a critical change in state tax law, and how two families are millionaires because of him. He spent his life in service to others on city councils, in the military, and in the state legislature, and it all started there on the parade ground at Fort Devon when he was a thirteen year old boy.

"You went there for a month," he explains. "They paid your way there and took you in. You put your clothes in a bag and you don't see 'em for a while. They give you a physical exam, and if you pass, they give you a uniform, and give you everything you're gonna need." His voice is authoritative, like a professor in a classroom rather than an elderly gentleman in his own home.

"They did something else that they couldn't do

today," he continues. "They'd brainwash you. After about an hour of close order drill in the sun, you'd go sit under a shade tree and an officer would come along with his crop and he was hitting his leather boots, and he would teach. About the government. All about the government, and all about the Army's general attitude in those days, ideology and so forth. They'd call that brainwashing today, but to me it was great. I had a good background through that alone just on how government worked." In that indoctrination, perhaps in an echo of the age, he heard a call to service and enlisted—at seventeen—in the National Guard. They put him in Company K of the 101st Combat Engineers.

As a teenager, he worked in a candy factory in his hometown of Woburn, Massachusetts, where he graduated high school in 1934—right in the middle of the Great Depression. "I came from a poor family," he explains, opening a drawer and placing two pens on his desk. "My family wasn't poor for a lack of anything but a man who wasn't a cripple. He worked every day of his life and he died when he was fifty four. They had their problems in those days too, but they didn't think much of that," and neither does he, if I believe his tone. Great Depression-era Americans were stoic, at least by modern standards—they bore the hardships of poverty and the lack of opportunities by scrapping for work and conserving what they had. To them hard work and sacrifice were nothing noble or idealistic—it was Tuesday, or Saturday, and they were a paycheck away from destitution…sometimes less.

Elmer Elwood, the patriarch of the Chase family, had a bum leg and so could only hold certain types of employment. He found good work at Western Union, where he worked every day, and extra hard on the holidays.

"In those days," Larry continues, "they didn't have cards to send, so everybody who worked for the Western Union had to work on the holidays. So we'd have a pancake dinner or something and he'd be working, to support his family." His tight smile almost conceals the pride and esteem he bears for his father. This tone, these words, the adulation in the subtext, bespeaks a man's respect for another man without any trace of a son's affection for a father. Perhaps this means nothing more than it sounds—that he sees his dad both as a man and a father, the two images coexisting.

Or perhaps Larry considers him more as a peer—he speaks very highly of his attributes, without sentimentality's amber glow. It's hard to think of a ninety year old gent as someone's son, and he seems unable to see himself in that role now. His father's example is clear, though. In a time when most everyone had it rough, Elmer had it especially hard with his disability and three children to support. He worked constantly in service—to use Larry's own term—to his dependents. His example took on the weight of virtue, and for Larry became a formula—a set of obligations and duties to support one's family and those needing care.

There are certain jobs I wouldn't take, and certain jobs you wouldn't take, for whatever reasons we hold—pride and self-importance not the least among the reasons we might turn down a job that seems below us. But Great Depression era folks had different words for those jobs: opportunity, and necessity. So when Larry's family moved to Somerville, Massachusetts, he took a job washing dishes at the Green Parrot Café in

Medford, just across the town line. He also worked as an electrical apprentice, learning about wiring and practical electrical engineering. Between washing dishes and working towards a trade, he saved the fifteen dollars to attend school part time at the Massachusetts Institute of Technology's Lowell Institute of Technology.

"I took a series of seminars," he explains, "either one night, or one day, or weekend seminars where a lot of technical people went." The programs were on electrical engineering, from basic wiring to the function of resistors. Some of it applied to his apprenticeship, some of it didn't, but it augmented his fundamental understanding of the science and opened a new door. "I decided when I was lying on my back with a four pound hammer and a star drill tryin' to drill a hole through a stone wall that there had got to be a better way to make a livin'," he opines. Just such an opportunity came in talking to a gentleman from New Hampshire.

"I met a guy who was working for...a transformer company out of Concord. (He) was just leavin', and said they needed a guy. I saw the guy, and got a job," he says quite matter-of-factly. If there was any debate in his mind at the time, any thoughts or concerns for his future or the move, he doesn't even suggest them now. That year Larry left home to work for the Davis Transformer Company next to the state prison, following an opportunity he thought might sustain him for awhile; it opened more doors than he imagined. In 1939 he took a leave of absence from the National Guard in order to move to Concord.

That was how Larry worked: making friends and contacts, building relationships and taking opportunities, and always being willing to learn new skills. Davis
164

Transformer Company rewound transformers, which is to say that they replaced the wiring inside the transformer boxes when they burned out. The work was preferable to drilling wiring holes through stone foundations, and gave him a chance to use his education. He explains of his job, "In those days, transformers were made with metal cores and wrapped with copper of different sizes. Lightning would burn them out, or overloading would burn them out, or they'd just wear out from age. And if they had the correct serial numbers, so they had the right kind of steel in 'em, we could take those transformers and rewind them." But technology changed and the new transformers were not repairable. "So the company was sold and I had a chance to come up here to this town and go into business with a different guy," who he had met through his work in the electrical industry.

That gentleman, Holland Stockwell, had a brother who lived just across the Connecticut River in Lebanon, New Hampshire. The brother rented Larry a room. That is how the man from Woburn Massachusetts came to the Hartford, Vermont area—following opportunity, even as it led him farther and farther from home. He explains it matter-of-factly, as though it was simply what needed to be done and he had no second thoughts. Perhaps this was the case—that he looked wide-eyed and expectantly to the future without a tinge of doubt; but not likely. In any event, he continues on with only a short pause to rearrange the pens on his desk.

"I got a loan on my insurance policy," he continues, "and joined right in. I worked for the Twin State Electrical Supply. That was 1939. I worked there until November 1940, when I went into the service." His old unit, the 101st Combat Engineers, was alerted that year, so he

165

drove to their offices and tried to reactivate himself as an electrical inspector. "They were very fussy and wouldn't take me again," he explains. "I was just married…I was fat, had glasses." He quite nonchalantly slips in that he got married as if I had known, moving right on to the complications of rejoining the service; there are likely quite a few personal details he remembers, but doesn't mention. His wife was Anna May Greigs; they wed in 1940, a year after he moved to the area. She was a waitress at the Mayfair Restaurant, in the economically stagnant White River Junction downtown. I ask about her, about how they met, and he seems generally surprised I'm interested.

Born in Italy, Anna May moved to White River Junction with her family as World War II set fire to Europe. After graduating from a secretarial school in Concord, she returned to White River Junction to make more money as a waitress—such was the nature of the time, when women's labor paid poorly but working in a railroad town restaurant could be comparatively lucrative. They met and married soon thereafter, and in 1945 had a daughter: Cheryl Chase.

Larry's skills and work ethic helped him secure a job in White River Junction, and his demeanor endeared him to his employers—there was something they must have recognized in him, something they could relate to. Sitting here listening to the stories unfold, I get the impression that he could have worked with a hoe or axe as easily as with papers and pens—that a man of his constitution would find work where there was work to be found, and excel at it.

The service reenlisted him, though he did not serve in the Guard much longer—Larry was drafted six months later, and though he tried to stay with the 101st Engineers, found himself enlisted in the regular Army. The colonel in charge of his Guard unit liked Larry, and Larry was dedicated to the Engineers, but the draft was for the regular forces; the colonel "gave me a letter saying that they'd like to see me back in the engineering corps," Larry explains. "I gave that to them...they put me to bed, and when I got up, they said 'you're in the Army!' I don't know what happened to the letter." He smiles; he'd been had, but keeps his humor about it. Despite his attachment to the Engineers, he dutifully became part of the regular Army, taking on a new role in the service: ferrying personnel from the east coast to destinations throughout the country.

Equipped with rail passes and vouchers, he rode the trains from White River Junction and Boston to South Carolina and Texas, shepherding new recruits and special personnel wherever they needed to go. Then new orders came down the line, for him to pack his warm weather gear and deploy to the Canary Islands to turn an airport into a US Army Air Corps base. But then "the supply guy up in Greenland got shot," he says, adding "friendly fire. They transferred me." Instead of the warm islands, he spent about a year on a frozen spit of land midway between America and England. The base was a waypoint for aircraft heading to Europe, and later, for personnel rotating back to the United States.

There was not much for Larry to do as the planes came and went and the days dragged on interminably. There is always something to do on an airbase, on a farm, or just about anywhere, for a man who likes to stay busy—a man such as Larry.

"I'd take a course," he tells me. "I qualified as a

flight mechanic. These here," he says, nodding to his medals in the shadowbox mounted to the wall behind him, "these are the Air Force (recognitions) for flight mechanics and so forth. You'd have to qualify for them, and study, and take tests. I qualified for probably half of those up there just to have something to do." Between the qualifications he earned, his previous service, and his age (which was, in his mid twenties, considerably older than many of the other draftees), he accumulated nearly forty service points; only twenty four were required to earn an honorable discharge.

Working came naturally to Larry, be it at the candy factory or washing dishes, learning the electrical trade or getting trained in aircraft mechanics. When he needed money, he found a way to make it; when he had free time, he found a way to fill it. His work ethic suited him well; Harold Wright might identify with him. Sitting idly, playing cards or shooting dice in the barracks never appealed to Larry and even now I don't notice many fiction books, video cassettes or DVDs, or the other trappings of idle leisure in his home. Elmer Elwood's example served his son well.

The Army needed a First Sergeant on base, so near the end of his duty in Greenland he was promoted. "That was one thing wrong with the rotation stuff," he observes. "They had so many first sergeants, and no more, and they had enough so that they didn't have to go overseas. So they made me a First Sergeant for about three months!"

Then a squadron came through on their way to the US, and the commanding officer on site told him to go home as part of their crew. He found his way back to Anna May in Hartford, and back to the old job Twin

168

State Electrical Supply kept for him—his loyalty runs deep, and his dedication was reciprocated, first by the National Guard colonel, then by Twin State Electrical Supply. The lieutenants in the CMTC had lectured all about loyalty, his Methodist religion preached dedication, and he watched, growing up, his father work diligently—their lessons greatly shaped his character, and that loyalty kept paying off.

In those days Larry sold electrical supplies—wire and conduit, switches and wiring boxes, the supplies contractors need for new construction. "They had the idea that electrical supplies would become the new thing," he says. "They weren't right. It wasn't. Electronic supplies, you can put a five-thousand dollar item in a little box this big and mail it. Five-thousand dollars worth of conduit would take three carloads. Electric supplies are like plumbing supplies, nuts and wires and bolts and so forth." He draws absentmindedly with his pen, the tip retracted so it traces inkless loops on the oak desktop. I keep noticing his pens—he keeps fidgeting with them.

Veterans could be recalled for up to a decade after serving, but he found a better way to serve his country than remaining a name in the back of a forgotten file cabinet: he joined the Civil Air Patrol, which is the civilian auxiliary of the Air Force. Though not technically a uniformed service department, in its own way his service with the CAP added to his eclectic service record. Meanwhile, he sold electrical supplies and deepened his connections to the Hartford Township villages. Being a salesman meant spending a majority of his week on the road, meeting clients and distributors, so he spent his time at home building ties with his neighbors and community.

"It wasn't until 1946 that I really started getting acquainted with the community—and even then I was gone three or four days a week," he says with what might be a hint of regret. He gradually increased his involvement with the Methodist Church in White River Junction, and branched out from there. Anna May was Catholic, and through her family and church connections he came to have friends in White River Junction's Italian community. By degrees he was becoming more and more a part of the community, despite being on the road so much.

His company's softball team was getting ready for a league game one spring evening, and Larry was all set to close up the books for the day and go join them when Holland Stockwell called him into his office. "He said 'Larry, I'd like you to fill in for me, I'm supposed to go to this meeting in Boston'," he says. Larry was looking forward to the game, but was presented, instead, with a major opportunity: to go to a representatives association meeting on his company's behalf. "I guess I looked a little perturbed. I said 'well, I think the team has a softball game tonight, I was supposed to play in that.' 'This is more important. It's an opportunity. I won't bother to talk about it now, I'll see you in the office in the morning, but I want you to attend the meeting tonight.' So I did." He pauses a moment to rearrange the pens on his desk, picking one up to use like a baton as he marks time through the rest of the story.

"And I was glad I did," he says in a cadence, "because right off the bat I was greeted there and they knew me. The next day at the office he said 'you're starting a new career. You're going to be busy, and if you're going to make something of yourself, you'd better enjoy it, 'cause if you don't enjoy it, you'll never be happy.'" These sage words, recalled through many decades, sound a little too polished, a little too—perfect. But this is a keystone memory, one of those that marks a turning point in Larry's life, and is necessarily dramatic. Many things are only as important as we make them; Larry made this moment, punctuated by that pen, monumental.

"'You want to make an effort now,'" he continues, still quoting his old boss, "'because you've reached a breaking point between yourself and your friends. Some you're going to keep, some you're not going to keep, they're moving and getting married. You've got an industry here where you're going to meet a lot of people. Make 'em your friends. Make it important to be at their meetings.'" He puts the pen down and allows a moment for his story to sink in.

That was the final measure that blurred the distinction between work and life—between business contacts and friends. This advice set him up for two careers, and with them, made him the man he is today. When he took it to heart, his perceptions changed: friends could be means to ends, and for a desired end there were means he could befriend. It was his official introduction into politics and the subtle art of manipulation—which I do not mean to tarnish his character, but to show a monumental revelation that changed the way he saw social politics. Larry went to their meetings, and he went to their conventions; he went to their parties, and he went to their retirement celebrations. Years later a guy he knew cornered him and joked, "you're the bane of my life Larry." Why, he asked. "Everyone tells me that you were at so-and-so's funeral and I wasn't there.

Now I have to go to all the funerals too!"

That level of personal attention, that connection to organizations and the people who run them, made him a welcome figure in local associations. The next big step in his civic involvement came when he joined the Veterans of Foreign Wars post in White River Junction; he knew some of the guys, and soon he rose to the fore in their social structure. "I did that for the VFW, go to their meetings and stuff, and met different guys around," he says with utter nonchalance. "The time that I belonged to the VFW became an opportunity," one he realized by increasing degrees. Again he uses that word, opportunity. "I was a salesman, but probably a poor one because I talked too fast. It was almost an addiction. I talked so fast you couldn't understand me. If there were two or three other people in the room, I didn't want to talk." But talking to groups in all manner of settings is part of being a leader.

"In the VFW, I had to talk. I got so I didn't care how many people where there, I just got up there and talked. I never studied it, I don't know, because I don't have that education, but I have a knack for understanding what the hell is going on. Sometimes it bores me stiff," but his life is a testament that even when the going gets boring, effective leaders keep going. He worked steadily through his aversion to public speaking; he worked to slow his rapid delivery, and build connections with different groups at various levels within the VFW. The experience he developed by representing Twin State Electrical Supply to many people from many backgrounds, and coordinating different groups of suppliers and consumers, came in quite handy for managing the VFW's affairs.

The VFW placed increasing trust in Larry, the just reward for gaining their confidence and serving the organization well. "Yeah," he confirms, "I was quite popular in that." He rose quickly through their ranks, all the way up to Post Commander. This put the man from Massachusetts in charge of his VFW post in Vermont, a position he regarded with due respect. As he speaks of it, though, he diminishes his importance and says nothing of his social affluence. What comes through clearly is how he regarded each task with the VFW as if it had the utmost importance. His service was careful and time consuming, but his dedication was acknowledged and appreciated. It comes, then, as no surprise how he rose from a general member to the Post Commander so quickly…and that Larry didn't stop there.

* * * * *

Korea, 1950: war erupts between the North and South. America joins South Korea, fighting a proxy war against the Soviet Union, which backed the North Koreans. Though already in the Civil Air Patrol, and in his forties, Larry was again drawn towards military service. He joined the Naval Reserves as an engineer—one of the Seabees. "They sent me to Dartmouth College for the inactive reserve," he explains. "I kept waiting for a call to go, 'cause when they came after me for the Seabee's, they gave me a commission." But he remained in Hartford, and six years later—well after the armistice that brought an uneasy peace to the 38th parallel—received his honorable discharge.

With that service, he had served in components of every branch of the United States military except the

Marine Corps. The shadowbox overhead holds Army and Navy insignia, qualification medals and a few tour of duty ribbons. I would not be surprised to hear he has a box somewhere full of incremental insignia, medals, and ribbons enough to make a Russian general blush. Though he never saw combat—for which he seems quite thankful—Larry certainly kept busy enough over twenty-some years of various service to earn his distinctions. His reenlistment during Korea galvanized his support in the VFW.

"I was always a guy who liked organizations, I liked government," he says with conviction. "I think it has a lot to do with the brainwashing in the CMTC." He doesn't shy away from that word, brainwashing, almost like he gets a kick out of applying such a complicated idea, such a dirty word, to his life; he credits their indoctrination with producing his social conscience and work ethic—and all that those traits brought him. Work and civil involvement are comfortable, familiar. Serving in the armed forces was also something of a family legacy, as his grandfather fought for the Union in the Civil War.

Yet for all the duty, honor, and other virtues inherent in his service, his years in the military also paid a second check that helped keep his finances secure against the sort of poverty he knew as a child. That security was a luxury to this Great Depression man, and something he cherished as an adult.

But poverty isn't the appropriate word for hard times now, he says, setting himself up for a diatribe. There's a feeling you get in a man's voice, in its power and speed, when he gathers strength to rail against the injustices of the world, and it's that feeling I have right now. The more he speaks, the faster he moves the pens, lifting one over the other and shuffling them quickly while his wife wanders past the doorway without looking in.

That old habit is still in there, that fast-talker trying to get a message out before something happens—before he loses his nerve? Or his audience? Or himself? Is there still, under all those medals and all those stories, a shade of insecurity—of that young man who wasn't comfortable speaking in public? Or is this the tired anger of an experienced politico who no longer confuses holding one's tongue with virtue? There are times and places, surely, when nothing below a good bellow or lashing is sufficient, and perhaps my audience is such an occasion.

"I always get a little bit upset with myself in my own ways," he says, "when I read in the paper about the people who live in poverty. People don't live in poverty. They may be poverty stricken, but when they're old enough to sign their names, they can get up to thirty-two, forty-thousand a year from the government. If children go hungry from want, like here in the Upper Valley, it's 'cause their parents are causing it. Either their parents are dopers, or drinkers, or drunkards, or whatever, they're taking the money that should be right, or they're too lazy to go down there and ask for help; or too proud." His tone dismisses the lot of them, cutting them down with a fearsome tone.

His eyes burn with a frustration that will come up again, I am sure. Larry has seen poverty, the check-to-check living where the difference between getting by and falling flat was one easily lost job in an era with no government welfare. It seems as if Larry wants to pump his fist and declare *and my father never complained!*, but instead he sits silently across the desk biting his tongue and biding his time.

Larry has empathy and charity for those who fail despite trying, but none for folks whose idea of work is imploring others to support them. "You look at some of these people that go to the Haven," he says, referencing the local homeless assistance center, "you see 'em outside smoking cigarettes and some of them have cars. How can you have money for cigarettes and cars and not for food?"

He supports organizations like the Upper Valley Haven—he just decries the mismanaged priorities of some patrons. The boozers, the dope addicts, the poor who have money for self-destructive luxuries but not for food...these are the specific recipients of his vitriol, painted simplistically and exclusively. I identify with Larry, and share the righteous indignation pouring from the mouth and steaming from the ears of this old man, all the while conscious that I'm agreeing with an over-simplification of images—an easy thing to do, and exactly what the conversation demands. The poor will always be with us, says a book nearly two thousand years old; still, neither of us have much use for the self-defeating.

We sit in silence in the eye of his tirade, thinking about *why*, and *what can be done*. The "homeless" with cars and growling bellies, complaining about cosmic injustice from nicotine stained lips...Larry considers them near the very bottom of society—an important distinction, if we are to know Larry at all. They are below a group he regards with paternal care: the working poor, to use his phrase—the ones he need not say remind him of his family during the Great Depression.

"Our biggest (concern) is the working poor," he continues with a tone much more caring. "I worry more about the working poor than about the others…there's a lot of working poor. I think people look at them and say 'Jesus, these people, if they make under twenty-thousand dollars, or whatever, they get all this free—Medicare, glasses, everything. And here I make forty thousand, I get nothing.' There are those who won't get up for work, and why should they do that when they can live for free? There is an answer to that, but you won't find a politician to do it!" He takes a moment to consider his next words.

This energy does not come from pure derision, which would make his rant scarcely worth more than a footnote, just the ramblings of a bitter old man; rather, his vehemence comes from honest concern over the plight of those he believes can be helped. Larry has been in their place, working to help support a family that needed every dime he earned, and has seen his family overcome those trying times. I can tell in his eyes, these flashes of compassion and anger from seeing opportunities wasted, that what fuels his passion—and anger—is a real desire to help…

…and the survivor's ego of one who has conquered a foe still besting other people. It is hard not to look down on those who fail, despite help, where you have succeeded on your own. He is less guilty of this than others, but not innocent. For that matter, neither am I.

Larry has a powerful social conscience and good intentions that are confronted, confounded and insulted by the sight of downtrodden people squandering the means they have and the help they get. Larry is not a mean man—he cares deeply, and is deeply frustrated.

177

Deep passion leads to passionate words, and deep wounds—especially for a man who sympathizes so strongly.

"You gotta have a system that says 'look, if you earn forty-thousand a year, we're going to let you keep thirty-two thousand,' or whatever, so that your income is going to increase because you went to work. There's yet to be a program where as you work your way in, you'll eventually get off, but they're not going to take you off the day you pass 'this' mark." While I agree, an awkward silence falls like a curtain between us; it will either lift for Act 2 or cut me off from Larry forever.

* * * * *

Working backwards from this tirade, I need to know if he ever did anything about these problems with welfare and taxes and government—if he was ever involved enough in creating solutions to infuse his indignation with righteousness…or if he's just another bitter old man yelling in the dark. My entire opinion, now, having watched the careful, reserved man come nearly unraveled, hinges on that central question.

This is a matter he has thought about—a lot, ever since he watched White River Junction's industry drop off after WWII. As the mills closed and the sidewalk rolled up, the unemployed appeared on doorsteps and sidewalks in alarming numbers. Many found work here and there, but neither as steadily nor as readily as in generations before. He felt inclined to do something for the sake of the township, but didn't know exactly what.

In 1955 Anna May passed away, and shortly thereafter he moved to this house on Wilder Street, on the hill high above Hartford. With the interstate a few blocks away, he could travel long distances and still be home at night…and in the evenings, become involved in the town government. That's where he found an opportunity to do something about the problems—and found even more problems to fix.

"The way things used to be here, everything was secret." He rearranges the pens again, looking at the desk, looking at me. "If you went to a meeting of the Board of Selectmen, you sat outside of the room until they called you in, and you walked in and they closed the door behind you, and when you're done, you left. No one else heard what you said. You couldn't bring any pressure on them. You couldn't bring a dozen guys with you," he says acerbically. "That's how it ran."

Each component village of Hartford—Wilder, White River Junction, Quechee, Hartford Village, and West Hartford—had their own Post Office and volunteer firefighters. They also each had their own schoolhouses for the lower grades, supported by miniscule tax bases. For all the homey feel of the small towns, for all the rural Vermont charm of the villages, they were not terribly effective at self-governance or much able to provide education. Between over-the-road trips with Twin State Electrical Supply and his evening meetings with the VFW, he pondered what more he could do within the community.

But wait—he just mentioned, a moment ago and merely by way of date-stamping his story, that his wife died. How did he raise their daughter? How did her death and his single parent lifestyle affect him? Larry glossed over all of this so well I nearly missed it. I ask about them, but he shuts me down. This is the story of the towns he's telling, and his role, and he is completely disinterested in leaving the formal to indulge the personal. I would love to see more of his humanity—of the rich and passionate character behind these facts and figures, but he is wholly uninterested in showing me that side. Perhaps it's too personal; perhaps no one ever much cared for it before, or, most intriguingly, perhaps he opened himself up too much once and was terribly hurt by it. I don't know, he's not telling, and speculation is a dangerous game; so, as Larry continues, on with the story…the way he wants to tell it.

"The story of my part, I was good at organization," he explains, calmly. "For some reason, I'm one of those guys who looks older and smarter than I am. I don't know if it's the bald head and the glasses or what it is…" He smiles affably, and here in his bearing, in his calm demeanor, is a guy I like; someone I trust. I'm still looking for the fuel in his fire, but I can't help pardoning his occasional flare-ups. Larry is likeable, and has an edge that suggests he actually does know more than you, and should be followed and agreed with, even before you hear his argument. This charisma influenced his life as much as his work ethic.

"When I got drafted," he says, "the guy made me the acting corporal to take the guys down to the office. When I get called to jury duty, the judge makes me the foreman of the jury. But that's the way it was. I get over into something, and speak my piece and say something, and the next thing you know I'm in charge of something. So I ran for a couple of offices." First, he tried running for the Board of Selectmen, in part to change their closed-door policies and back room politics. "I just got the urge to run," he says, humbly.

Larry ran as a Republican, as "I favor what used to be Republicanism. But I can see both sides, and I can see why some people get rabid about it." That fits—Larry seems to be in favor of economic self-determination, and private organizations (such as Haven) providing social services rather than the government. Vermont was predominantly Republican for decades, until the definitions of the parties slowly inverted; the same values that made Vermonters Republicans in the nineteenth century makes many of them "liberals" today; it will change again. By understanding a bit about this label, one of few he attaches to himself, perhaps I can see— and show—him more clearly.

Where I find trouble reconciling the man with my understanding of twentieth century Republican politics is how he was eager to see the joining of the smaller, autonomous villages into the town of Hartford. There was significant benefit in consolidating their public resources, but Republicans have long advocated smaller government and more autonomy for citizens, cities, and states—the antithesis of which is incorporating small villages into one town. Yet his rationale—that combining the villages would improve their overall education, fire protection, and other infrastructures—makes a case stronger than arguments for maintaining village autonomy. Between the Republican ideology of small government and his work towards the Democratic idea of central governmental entities unifying the villages into something more, there's a measure of ideological conflict that shows a fierce independence which feels so quintessentially "Vermont."

His alliance with a long-standing national party didn't help in his first bid for office, though. The former

Postmaster ran against him, and as he had been a public figure for quite awhile, had the name recognition to beat Larry. Daunted but not dissuaded, Larry refocused his energy within the VFW and bided his time for another run at public office.

Meanwhile, he was invited to join a social circle of sorts: the Phoenix Club, an organization of investors who enjoyed a good drink as much as a good stock tip. They met monthly, each time at a different member's home, to manage a group portfolio and enjoy each other's company. Among them Larry found camaraderie and support from all across the economic spectrum. Through his studies, military and public service, work, and living in three states, Larry has been exposed to a lot of different kinds of people and ideas. The Phoenix Club was eclectic and stimulating enough to capture his interest and earn his devotion.

"I have this knack for understanding, I understand people," he said just a minute ago. "I'm very good with people, I don't know why. They trust me for some reason. It's the way it is now." Even today, sitting here in his home, he is gaining my trust and respect at an unusually quick rate—I am trying hard to maintain my objectivity. This is part of Larry's charm—he can identify, or at least interact well, with people of all sorts and kinds. His greatest skill is using his affability to form relationships, which he honed through the Phoenix Club.

"Over the years those guys have been everything from lawyers, plumbers, excavators, doctors..." he says. "There's only fifteen of 'em but they get together and argue and fight and drink and play poker." They come from all demographics; a little cross section of

White River Junction. "And every time we get a new guy, they're 'oh we don't want him in here, we don't know anything about him,' and if he doesn't fit, he doesn't fit, he leaves. I got to know a lot of guys that way. You'd meet a guy with a different way of life, different ideas," he explains, opening his desk drawer and looking through a series of hanging files. Meeting such a range of people seems, in and of itself, a benefit of the organization; I can hear that between his words, see it in the way he shapes his thoughts. He was once one of the new guys they didn't trust, but he won them over. Larry seems truthful, and perhaps they identified with that; he seems trustworthy and stoic—perhaps they connected with that. Perhaps they came to think of him as one of them, a Vermonter—I am beginning to see how that would fit as well.

Not finding what he wants, or finding nothing that he might want, he closes the drawer. I wonder if he's been fidgety his entire life, or if this is how his old rapid speaking habit manifests itself nowadays...or... He is about to say something, but then does not, looking neither lost nor perplexed—simply modest, a man on the border of saying too much and fearful of crossing over.

A few of his friends in the Phoenix Club he knew from the VFW—they helped him get elected to a national office within the organization. "That," he says with renewed energy, "was another one of my pleasant experiences. I was the Commander of the 1st District of the VFW, which was Maine and New Hampshire and Vermont. Now they changed it, I think because of me," but he keeps talking about VFW districts and zones and not why they would have changed the districts because of him—it seems another case of modesty, though there is a fine line between his modesty and pulling punches.

Larry doesn't couch his convictions, his support of the armed services, or his denouncing of the self-defeatists among the poor. While he does not tell me everything—he has yet to mention meeting or marrying Philomena, his current wife, and said nothing more about his daughter Cheryl than that she was born—what he says sounds heartfelt and feels earnest. Larry is a man of consummate diplomacy, well tempered in politics, his stories belying almost no trace of evasiveness, pandering, or acting...or personal details. Perhaps this is a factor of his age and the years; perhaps his perspectives have assumed the weight of law, leaving no room for self-doubt. In any event, the sun is coming at a steeper angle through his window now as his narrative turns once again to White River Junction.

"I got interested in the town," he says, "and there were things in that town (politically) that would benefit our business." These things would help other businesses as well, especially in light of the exodus across the bridges to New Hampshire's lower tax rates. "I served on a couple committees for the town to go over the tax systems and so forth. I served as the chairman of the, I don't know, they had a program where the government would come in and tear down old buildings and build up the land..." the Urban Renewal Project. "We had that going...and then the town voted it down." His words fall off slightly, losing the energy that connects his thoughts.

With that project sidelined, he focused on repealing the capital interest tax. "Companies had to pay a tax on their stock in trade," he says, straightening his
184

shoulders, hopping the pens one over the other. That tax added incredible drain to their existing overhead, especially for those dealing in low-markup, high-volume business. "There were several wholesalers in town," and other businesses that made money in volume deals. "That tax was based on everybody being a farmer. The wealth was judged on what they own," which included unsold merchandise and unsold stock options. Capital fundraising campaigns that involved selling stock options started far in the red.

"They said we couldn't do it," couldn't repeal that part of the tax. "They said the people wouldn't go for it. We looked around, found a couple other towns that did it, got the information, made up the brochures, and passed 'em around. Come time of the election, it passed, and we didn't have that tax anymore. They still had the tax on equipment, but they didn't have the tax on stock." That eased some of the financial burden on local businesses, but its benefit was promptly mitigated when Vermont passed the state sales tax.

"That drove just about everybody out of town," he says solemnly; business left White River Junction and crossed the river to New Hampshire, or, like the mills, went down south where labor was cheaper. "When you were in competition with somebody across the bridge in New Hampshire, and they didn't have that tax—the sales tax—right off the bat, you're five percent more expensive than they are."

As the businesses moved or folded, they left behind a city with sharply increasing unemployment and falling economic resources. Many of the businesses that lingered were built right along polluted waterways, filthy from a century's worth of dye, sewage, and industrial runoff. Larry used his growing influence to do what he could for the businesses, and for the rivers through town. Working to help the villages came as naturally as working during high school to help the family, and joining the service to help his country; at each of these stages, truth be told, he also helped himself.

On the verge of a story about the polluted rivers, he detours onto his favorite Biblical passage. Though a sidetrack, it is not a distraction, for it offers a glimpse into the formative theology he has yet to discuss... but nonetheless, apparently has its effects. The story is that of Jeremiah, which he retells to me from his own understanding.

"That's the story of the king's cupbearer," he narrates with a certain air of nobility and importance unheard in his words before. "He came from a rich family. The Arabs came and Jerusalem was ransacked, the temples were torn down, and the gates were smashed.... One night he had a conversation with the Lord, and...I can hear the Lord saying 'Jeremiah, you come from a good family, you have the king's ear, you're a big shot. Why don't you do it? Why do you keep asking me to do it, you do it.' So he did, and went to the King...and he went into Judea and got people who knew how to repair gates and do this and that. He got people that could plow, (gathered) the merchants back together. They rebuilt."

I can easily see Larry reading that biblical passage about Jeremiah every so often by lamp light late at night, an alarm clock set entirely too early, smiling and chuckling quietly as he thumps the pages with his thumb. But this is only half of the story, and his fortitude would be half as impressive were it not for how he failed in his first campaign, were it not for

186

those in the shadows who shook their heads derisively at the man from Massachusetts trying to inject himself into Vermont politics. Without opposition, Jeremiah's struggle would be neither as inspiring nor as credible. There were those who ran against Larry, denounced his ideas, who opposed him with that mixture of facts and their own inventions that people use to disagree. And so he continues with the rest of the story, the part with which it seems he identifies the most.

"In the meantime the people in the other cities got mad about this, because he was taking workers away from them. He was going to be competitive to them, and they sent a message to him that said 'you're wasting your time, these people are going to go back again and the city's going to fall again. You're wasting your money and wasting your time. Why don't you come down to the village of Nono and discuss this?' Now that's in the Bible. And they have a great success and a great feast, but that stopped me right there: I thought 'Nono.' Every place I've ever been, every committee I've ever been on, everything we tried to do I thought was good, there was always some bastard that says 'no, no!'" And so with humor and a flicker of fighting spirit, he smiles and returns to the story he previously aimed to tell.

He was one of the founders of the Green Mountain Economic Development committee, "which is still going and doing a helluva job for us here," he says. "I just liked that stuff, so I got heavily involved. Too much in some cases. I got started because there were plans to build a dam, probably half a mile below here." The federal government's plan called to build a dam below Hartford that would have flooded much of the upper Connecticut River Valley, threatening White

River Junction and other local interests. It would have produced power for the twin states and larger markets beyond, competing directly with the power plant in the Wilder Dam just above Hartford.

"It was going to put some of the utility companies out of business up here. So we formed the Connecticut River Watershed Council," he says. "I was the vice president for Vermont. Green Mountain Power talked me into that, and I didn't think it would be much but it became quite a burden." This is all he says of the trouble—that it was a burden, but not how or why before he goes on and tells me more about the organization.

They established representation for the watersheds along every river that fed into the Connecticut in the state of Vermont; they developed some clout; but this doesn't help me understand Larry terribly much. I hold onto the story for its value in chronicling the history of White River Junction—here, its flirtation with being intentionally flooded—but struggle again to find the man under the headlines. His stories are factual rather than personal; his self-history, the narrative piecing together his self-understanding, is inextricable from committee names and formal history as if the person is hiding behind the accomplishments and only comes out in the occasional tirade. I would love to get a few drinks in him and get him going, but unfortunately I don't see that happening.

In addition to protecting the watersheds from flooding, the Watershed Council also worked with businesses along the rivers to stem pollution and clean up the waterways. "Notice when people built a town," he says, "they built with the backs of the buildings to the rivers when the rivers should have been beautiful. The rivers were a source of disposal, everything went into the rivers. After a while, the rivers got pretty clogged up. But more than that, the land itself got clogged up." Therein lay a problem for Hartford: Hartford Village fronts on the Connecticut River and is separated from White River Junction by the White River; Wilder is a few yards uphill from the Connecticut; the Ottaquechee River flows along the western edge of Quechee, a nearby village. They were built around the waterways, right along them, so increasingly foul water brought increasing health risks.

Vermonters have particularly strong, often ancestral, connections to the land; Larry's connection to the land was through a concern over water-use business, and about protecting the natural beauty of the waterways that cut through his towns…and the health of the people who lived alongside them. He spoke up and joined many native Vermonters in the movement.

Larry had no training in ecology, so he involved ecologists in the Watershed Council to draw up management plans. Then he met with business owners and boards of directors to get their support, which he gathered rather easily. "The people who wanted to help us were the industries along the river," he says. "They were dumping mostly dyes into the river, nothing to worry about, it just colored it. The towns would bitch like hell, though. They didn't want us around, 'cause they were dumping raw sewage into the river!" The old fire is back; it takes self-victimization and raw sewage to get him going, but he can work up a glorious froth.

"You go to the different mills," he says cresting and backing down a bit, "and there was a lot of 'oh yeah, we'll do whatever you want us to, we'll put in a plant to try to clean that stuff up more.'" The mills were onboard with the cleanup, but the biggest polluters—the towns they were trying to improve by protecting the rivers—were their loudest critics. "It was kind of funny that it just backfired on the whole thing!"

Then Larry, man of politics, man of organization, father and civic organizer, ran for state office. In 1981 he ran for a seat in the Vermont House of Representatives, and won handily. "Twice in my life I guess I was proud," he explains. "First time I ever took the oath of office in the Army I was proud. And when I took the oath of office in Montpelier I was proud." He leans back and squares his shoulders, obviously pleased to lay a claim that only a small percent of folks can ever stake.

"Beautiful place," he says, eyes misting up a bit on this late afternoon emotional roller coaster. "The big shots make you guarantee you're going to do this and going to do that, serve the people, serve the constitution, protect the state. And then they recess, eyes full of tears. Each party goes to their separate rooms. And the first thing they do, they've already elected their officers before they even get there, the first thing they do when they get there," his words begin to clunk heavily through the air, suddenly naked, without pride or comfort or anything to suggest that he enjoys saying them, "they have someone from the national party come in and give us a couple hour lecture on what we can do with our power to make ourselves elected again." The mist in his eyes might be nostalgia, or pride, or, maybe a lingering disenfranchisement.

The chairmen of committees, regardless of their effectiveness or qualifications, get shuffled every time one party comes into power—the Democrats kick the

Republicans out and vice versa. When the voting starts, the fur really flies, and at first Larry was genuinely ignorant. "Dumb me," he says, "I didn't want to look and see if they were Democrats or Republicans, I wanted to know if the bill was good." The illusion the voters hold is that they elect men who will vote for the good propositions and against the bad ones, representing the will of their constituents with every vote they cast—it is a logical ideal…and a nice daydream. The reality of party politics rather shocked Larry Chase. Laying them bare here, he's turning my stomach as well.

"So I had a bunch of people sign on (to my bill). Well, a couple days later, all these nice guys come up and say 'Larry, I'm sorry, I can't sign onto that thing.' 'Why not? What's wrong with it, we can change it.' 'No, it's a party bill. We don't want the Republicans to get credit for that; we don't want them to get blamed for that.' All the guys looked at it and said it's a good bill, but they couldn't vote for it!" His brow furrows, and he tries to cross his arms but lays his hands upon the desk instead. "The first time my party told me that, I said 'you can let me vote for who I want to, or you want me to stop coming to caucus?'"

That's fantastic idealism, but tastes a little too good to be true. I ask if there were ever times that he went with the party line and voted for bills he didn't support, or voted against those he did. "Yes," he said. Those cases, he explains, often involved gaining political support for bills and initiatives he was trying to pass, where voting for someone else's bill would garner their support for his. The feeling of voting against his conscience for political ends as he blithely followed a system he opposed must have been strange, the dissonance immense, for the man who was used to being a leader and defending his convictions. The Commander of the VFW, in Montpelier, followed other men to vote in ways he didn't like.

Contradicting one's beliefs with actions does not sit well with most people—especially not Larry Chase. When he could, he voted with his conscience regardless of party distinctions, and he solicited support from anyone he thought might agree with his bills. Perhaps it was an act of purification, to take the high road as often as possible, to absolve himself of the occasional low road vote. Larry believed in using his power as he felt it was needed, to fix problems and protect people's interests; but then he fell into the mire of voting for reasons unrelated to the bill at hand. The same noble attitudes that garnered support in the VFW, the same principled drives that he used to carve a successful life for himself and his families, here put him in conflict.

Yet he kept diligently coming back, serving three consecutive terms between 1982 and 1988—the year he passed two milestones.

Like any natural resource, Larry's time was finite, and he had to choose priorities among his obligations. In addition to the councils and boards, he was still employed, and still serving as the Commander of the Veterans of Foreign Wars. "You think politics around here are bad," he taunts, "you should see the politics in an organization like the Legion or the VFW!" But there is no animosity in his voice now; only humor born of frustration checked by the observation that, for all its flaws, the system nonetheless manages to work.

"I spent three years with them," he says. "You had to give about a third of your time, and you had to belong to state government or some big company that would pay your way—you had to have some backing for that." Twin State Electrical Supply was accommodating, as was the Vermont Legislature, but he could only serve so long.

At seventy-two Larry was happily married, a former state representative, a member of the Board of Civil Authority and a Justice of the Peace, the chair of several committees and organizations, a father, and the president of a corporation: the one resultant from an earlier merger of Twin State Electrical Supply with Arrow Electronics. He was as connected to the town and region as he could be and still have time to sleep. If connections and public service suggest belonging, then he truly belonged to Vermont…but it was time to realign his duties and focus on his family.

In 1988 he left office and retired from Twin State Electrical Supply—two very important milestones in one pivotal year. "I made two men millionaires," he says, this time with a bit more rye in his grin. Business and the government took care of Larry, but for all his work with causes greater than himself, his physical wealth is modest. He seems comfortable, though, and enjoyed some very special opportunities over the years.

President George Bush Sr. visited Dartmouth College while in office, visiting the campus just three miles north of Larry's home. The local Republican organizations threw a cocktail reception afterwards. A colleague introduced Larry to the President, introducing him as an esteemed and recently retired state representative. President Bush smiled and shook Larry's hand while a photographer snapped their picture.

Larry downplays the story, but I fix on the meeting:

it's no small deal to be introduced to the President, nor is it any small matter to have so much behind an introduction.

"My brother used to call me," he says with an earnest but failed attempt at modestly, "a big frog in a small puddle." It is the first time his modesty has really failed today, which makes it seem all the more authentic.

A while later Larry dropped in to see Buddy Romano, a friend from the Phoenix Club who at the time was the budget director at the Urban Renewal Office... and a staunch Democrat. "I said to him one day, in his office," Larry narrates, "'when are you going to put the President's picture up? This is a government office, you're supposed to have the President up, regardless.'"

Then as a joke, Larry found the picture of him shaking hands with President Bush, slipped it in an envelope, and brought it in to Buddy. "I said 'here, I feel sorry you haven't got any pictures of the President for your wall, so I bought one for ya.' Next thing I know, he has it framed up on the wall, and it stayed there until he died. First thing his wife did was take that picture and bring it back and give it to me, thought I might like to have it," and he chuckles. "I still got it down in the cellar."

Larry is well respected in White River Junction, even by those opposite his party—this comes from a life of remembering names and showing respect. He will help you if he is able, or will point you to someone who can; he's helped businesses and a lot of people, and offered his support when he couldn't offer assistance... and he went to a lot of funerals. But when I ask him about how the town shows him their respect, about what that means to him—and other personal questions—he shies away.

Several times now I've tried to get him to answer personal questions, including a few about his family, and very quickly each time he segued onto other topics. I asked about Philomena, and he spoke about the Italians in White River Junction—they had an enclave on South Main Street, and several of them owned little grocery stores along the way, was all he said. Questions about Anna May were mostly fruitless, as he mentioned they met at the Mayfair and that she had previously been a secretary, but then he talked about the declining job opportunities in White River Junction.

Perhaps he shuns personal questions out of humility, the same humility that keeps his stories from sounding like stump speeches or braggarts' tales. Or perhaps, he best knows himself and his own life story in terms of organizations and associations and the service he gave. Then to know Larry Chase would not mean knowing the man, but knowing the company he kept and the actions he took. I can't say that I understand Larry Chase, but I do know him in exactly the ways he wants me to know him.

The facts are all here, deceptively straightforward, as I wonder in the afternoon's fading light about the inner workings of the man seated before me. The room is growing chilly and dark, and by my figuring we have come through eighty years in three hours and have only a decade to go. Night is coming into the room by degrees, so Larry turns on a lamp. There is only a short time left, and I still have a few more questions.

But then he drops one of his own. "So what do you think?"

I think that he gets satisfaction from completing a

task, and happiness from working with people he was often proud to call his friends. I think that politics and civil service were nearly as good to him as he was dedicated to them, providing him a lifetime of friends, auxiliary income, esteem and opportunity. I think he guards his personal life a little too well. I say something to this effect, anyway, and conclude how Larry Chase defines himself in terms of his associations with others; it confuses the hell out of him. He pauses a moment, fidgets with a few papers, and then strikes upon a story.

"We have a lot of volunteers at the Bugbee Senior Center," one of the organizations he still assists. "It does them (the volunteers) good, too. I can think of one person especially. This woman took care of her husband for five or six years after the onset (of his cancer). She was a mess. She looked twice her age, slumped over... when he died, I didn't know what was going to happen to her. She came down to the Bugbee a couple times, and they talked her into doing something. First thing you know, she's helping with the tables and doing this, then she changes her clothes and her hairdo, and now she's down there every day waiting on tables! It helps (the volunteers) too." It's the perfect parable for Larry, who spent his life working for others, and for causes greater than himself...all the while enjoying the various rewards of service.

Is this his essential nature, or was there something in the town that inspired his service? Would he have joined such organizations or run for office anywhere else?

"I would have been as involved elsewhere if I could have," he says. "There's more to do in town and not enough people to do it. I had the opportunity here to do it; whether I would have been able to do that in a bigger place, I have no idea. I think perhaps I would have been interested, because that's my background, I'm interested in that stuff."

Even as he retired from formal organizations, he joined new social circles. There is a breakfast club, of sorts, with whom he became acquainted as he found himself awake earlier and earlier with no place to be for longer and longer. On those early mornings he went to Crossroads, a restaurant on Sykes Avenue in White River Junction, and over coffee talked politics with the regulars.

"You can get one helluva breakfast there for seven dollars," he says, adding, "the place is usually mobbed in the morning. The families come in, the kids come in, and you get a good meal."

With good breakfasts available elsewhere, it is the people who keep him coming back to Crossroads. After withdrawing from the Phoenix Club, the morning ritual became all the more important. "I quit all the stuff at night," he explains. "First of all, I want to be here. Secondly, I'm not really fit to drive at night, especially if I get caught in a rainstorm. I can't see the sidelines of the road at night. My wife's ninety two, and I'm ninety," and her health has been sliding precipitously of late. That impression I've gathered from spare mentions he made, and how, later, he declined another interview on account of needing to take care of Philomena. At ninety, family is finally co-opting business and politics.

Philomena started coming with him to Crossroads, where a curious thing happened that illustrates his place in local society. "I told 'em, 'I've got to kind of relax things here and pay more attention to my wife, I'm going to bring her with me, and I understand you guys really don't want to tell dirty jokes in front of her, and I'm sure she wouldn't mind, but you can't do it. And so, we're going to sit by ourselves,'" he explains, laying it out to me as if I were on the stool next to him at the breakfast counter. "'No problem, no trouble,' they said, so I go in there and we sit at a booth, and within fifteen minutes there's seven, eight more chairs in a circle around. That's the way it is."

Even after he bowed out of the Phoenix Club and business and civic organizations, pulling quietly away, he keeps up his volunteerism at the Bugbee Senior Center and holds court at the Crossroads. He is an accomplished man—a big frog—with medals on his wall and memorabilia in his basement, and has done well; every man needs rest, and his is well earned.

So he folds his hands, our interview at its end. The room is cool, the sun having set. With the lamp and these final stories, I am literally seeing Larry in a different light. He shaped White River Junction and the Town of Hartford, serving Vermont and dozens of local organizations—and they shaped him. Larry is a Vermonter, as invested in the state and changed by it as anyone born there.

He looks older now than hours before, and somehow wiser, with the lamp light deepening the creases on his face. I feel more like a student than a friend, less like a biographer and more like a wide-eyed child learning about life; I'm reminded of that boy from Woburn so long ago sitting under a tree on the edge of a parade ground reverently listening to a wise instructor…and wonder if I've been brainwashed, too.

Top: Dot Jones in her dining room, in the home where she was born and would pass away in December of 2010.

Bottom: From left to right are Lorna Ricard, the author, and Dot, pictured at the "Cuba Libre?" photo exhibition at the Main St. Museum in White River Junction.

Dot Jones
In a Vermont State of Mind

The old school sits atop a springtime-green knoll midway up one of the Green Mountains in Hartford Village, on an open lot surrounded by trees and houses. Out back from the two-story brick building is the edge of a forest with birch and hemlock and maple climbing away from the playground up, up towards the ridge line. Leading from the front down, across that green knoll, is an asphalt walkway where once the ground was trampled bare by a steady stream of children, teachers and parents. The asphalt leads down to a home-lined street pointing southwest towards the White River. The sun set just to the left of this path, following over the children's heads as they bounded home. This was a Vermont country school, kindergarten through eighth grade, with wood paneling that traced the hallways far above the children's heads. When they grew taller than the wooden trim they were ready to move on to Hartford High, several miles nearer the morning sun.

The front door that towered so mightily over the children is buried now, bricked over with their seams outlining the old doorway, sealing it shut the way you can see the shapes from times gone by but can't go back yourself. The original playground was cut by half in the 1950s to make way for more classrooms, but a side playground is still there and accessible through a wooden archway in a picket fence. The children have been gone for a long time, but the building still casts its afternoon shadow over a flowerbed in their old playground. Within the flowerbed's wooden circle are stakes bearing the faded names of different flowers that still grow among the weeds. Children's squeals and screams once preceded them through the halls at recess and after school. Now, the shrill sounds inside come from drills and radial saws—the old school is becoming new offices for Health Care Rehabilitation Services of Southeastern Vermont.

The foreman, Richard, remembers the day his brother came bounding up the footpath and tried to catch the front door before it shut him out. He managed to get one hand around the door as it slammed, severing a finger and trapping his glove. "He ran home and got stitched up, and was back that afternoon," Richard said. "He found his glove by the doorway, and it still had his finger in it!" So many of Hartford's adults have memories of this place; so many grew up inside; thankfully, not many were maimed.

* * * * *

Dorothy Mock Jones lives in the Howard homestead, up a steep knoll from Route 4 just outside the edge of Hartford Village. She grew up there, returned to it after half a lifetime away, and it remains the only place she can imagine herself spending the best years of her retirement. "I was born in that room," she told me, pointing over my shoulder to a bedroom just around the corner from a massive cast-iron heating stove. Her grandfather built this homestead upon a working farm and tended it well into his golden years, before joining several generations in the Hartford Cemetery along the highway into town. Her mother Doris Howard married Lester Mock, the son of a long line of factory workers originally from Pittsburgh; he worked at a fabric mill in town. Lester moved into the Howard homestead and started his family in the same house where Doris was born. Dorothy Mock and her brother Richard, one year younger, grew up as the second generation of Howards born and raised in the homestead, living together with their grandparents, aunts, uncles, and cousins—three generations under one roof.

If smiles could twinkle, hers certainly would and almost does. Her blue eyes are mischievous, like those of a wily big sister—eighty-five years have only strengthened her spark. We sit on the same side of a large oak dining room table, enjoying a fantastic view of the White River from the window in the next room. A china cabinet sits in a far corner of this spacious dining room, protecting dishes, plaques, and totems. One commemorates her forty years of service to the Bellows Falls school system; another is a poem. In the next room, across a sea of white carpet, stand antique tables with ashtrays full of half-smoked cigarettes. A terrier prances around smelling things that have smelled the same for decades—Nelly is her name, and she sleeps upstairs in a kennel in Dot's bedroom.

There is another member of the household, a dear friend of Dot's from days gone long by: Lorna Ricard, who lives upstairs as well. Lorna breezes through the dining room occasionally, augmenting Dot's stories or sitting quietly in the next room smoking and talking about their mutual friends and adventures. Where Dot is short and slight, Lorna is a few inches taller and stronger.

They both smoke and both have the same sort of intense, piercing gaze that tells you someone of intelligence is trying to figure you out. But where Dot's smile is coy, Lorna's is straightforward—like their words. Dot tells stories and Lorna interjects concrete facts from the living room. Dot smiles more, but together they make me feel welcome. Their hospitality keeps the rooms warm and inviting, though their guests are fewer every year.

Dot was born on September 26th, 1921, during the fall harvest when the cornfields were half-picked and the squash were fat on the vine. Chickens roamed the acreage, and below the family's massive barn was a pigsty full of swine rooting through the cow manure. While she enjoyed living on the farm—it was all she knew—she looked forward to school even more. "They had one right up here," Dot tells me. "There was the Hawthorne family that lived there, and that was about it." Mrs. Hawthorne was the schoolmarm. "My mother said 'I don't want you to go up there, you will not meet enough people, you will not, no, you'll be in a bubble...' It would have been just Richard and I and them. Even I, as young as that, knew that I wanted more than that in school." Instead, she walked that country mile to the Hartford Village School—with its finger-stealing door—accompanied by her brother Richard after finishing their morning chores.

Dot remembers her first grade teacher, Myra Davis, "oh she was a witch!" and trying not to fall asleep. "Listen," Dot tells me now, seventy-some years after those memories, "we could read early. You know how boring that was, to know how to read? You still had to sit there and listen to people teaching you how to do it!"

She had a distinct advantage over the other children in grade school thanks to her mother, her aunt Florence, and the unconventionally well-educated women of the Howard family. Her grandmother graduated high school in the 1800s when few women even attended higher level grades, and Florence earned a full scholarship to the University of Vermont—which she declined in order to marry a college graduate. Her aunt Helen Howard was also a teacher. Dot was raised with a certain degree of intellectual privilege not common in early twentieth century rural Vermont.

Attending the Hartford Village School was a special privilege, one her mother worked hard to make available for her children; other children outside of the Hartford villages studied in one-room schoolhouses under the tutelage of local mothers, like the one Dot and Richard avoided. "I'm glad that my mother said 'no, I want them to be educated,'" she says. That education went farther than Doris Howard probably imagined.

When not in school she helped around the farm, guiding their field horse as it cultivated the cornrows. "I had to get up on the horse," she explains, "and my father would be plowing. I would make sure to go between (the rows), so the horse wouldn't step on the corn." The scene sounds romantic, straight out of a postcard, but she laughs at this notion.

"I didn't find that very much fun," she says, eyes twinkling with mirth. "It was hot, and the bugs were around. We didn't have a saddle, I just got up on the horse." Farming didn't appeal to her, as it hadn't for her father the mill worker. "My father was not a farmer, he didn't know a pig from a cow!" she jokes with an easy laugh. He still had his jobs on the farm, though, and so did she. While Dot didn't much fancy agriculture, she developed a healthy respect for hard work—from it she grew strong in body and spirit.

When the Great Depression hit in 1929, her family was less affected than many others across the country. Because they grew most of their own food and could always sell a bit of excess, they did not fear quite so powerfully for life as they knew it. Additionally, her mother worked at Colodny's Department Store in White River Junction, a job she held throughout the Depression years. Her mother's job "made it nice during the Depression," Dot explains. "That was a pretty bad thing, the Depression. Not for us, though," she confides, citing her mother's work and their production on the farm as the difference between scraping by and living comfortably. The Howard and Mock families held their own during trying times, persevering with their farm and Doris's city job while thousands of others lost their homes—and their hope. Coming of age in these times shaped her confidence and self reliance.

"I liked to work, and I didn't mind if they said to go hoe the garden," she explains. After the chores were done and her homework was completed to her grandmother's satisfaction, she and her brother Richard retreated to the enormous barn behind the house. There, nailed to the wall, was the steel hoop that changed her life.

"Inside, the barn was huge, huge, huge," she says slowly, wistfully, walking through its cavernous interior once more in her mind. "Three stories…bigger'n two or three houses!" The open space inside rivaled high school gymnasiums, Lorna observes on one of her trips through the dining room on her way to somewhere. Though time and distance grow memories as surely as rain grows watermelons, the barn is gone and there is no way to prove that it wasn't every millimeter as grand as they remember. "My brother and I put a hoop up in the barn," where they learned to play basketball above the pigsty. "We played hour after hour..." she recalls, dragging the vowels out reverently. To borrow her own word, basketball became her salvation.

It saved her from life as a farmer and enabled her to travel. She observes, "You get to travel all over with basketball. I went more places..." before trailing off modestly. We sit in a grand home, which she has shown me without showing off; she mentions that she traveled, trailing into a private thought without bragging about where. Her ability to tell without boasting is familiar from my afternoon with Harold Wright; her love of basketball, though, is quite unique to Dot. She made a four-decade career out of the sport; it enabled her to explore new opportunities, and live life on her own terms—a need which is easy to relate to. But perhaps "saved" is not the right word, even if she uses it herself.

Perhaps she means salvation more in the sense that basketball empowered and enabled—two very different concepts—her to attend college, led her to and through a forty year career, and brought her as far west as St. Joseph, Missouri. Richard was a star athlete; he helped her with layups and three-pointers, and while she learned the footwork to get around him, she was developing the skills and the love of competition that took her through high school on the Hartford High women's basketball team...and straight to Posse College on a basketball scholarship. The tenacity she developed sustained her through trying jobs and the challenge of being among the small (but growing) number of women to attend college—especially on a sports scholarship.

That was not an easy ticket to punch, nor were the days sweating in a foul-smelling barn perfectly idyllic. Yet she speaks of playing basketball on the wooden barn floor and competing on her college team with euphoric nostalgia. Indeed, to know Dot is to know her love for sports and competition, and to respect her dedication to education.

She says Richard was "a star athlete." Her brother played baseball and football, basketball and other sports for Hartford High, and taught them to his sister on their farm there along the White River. He never went easy on her—she wouldn't have it—and as he learned new sports, he shared them. "My brother was a great golfer," Dot explains with a tone both reverent and still a tad envious.

"I said 'well, this must be fun,' so I played along." Golf became a lifetime sport they shared from youth until his death several years ago. The competition excited her, as much for the chance to compete against others as for the nature of competing against herself; golf also gave her another way to spend time being active outside in the mountain air.

"I never was an expert at (golf), but I could hit it! I wanted to hit it a country mile," she says, catching herself suddenly, "but I never got...no, I would not call myself outstanding in golf. But I like to play!"

She also sang in the high school choir and joined clubs to socialize with as many people as she could—to develop friendships and meet people outside of her life on the farm, she explains. Interacting with other kids, especially those older than she, was a selling point of the Hartford school over the schoolhouses; she made the most of her opportunities. These were the elements that honed young Dorothy Mock and set her on course through a novel life itself as quirky and charming as the woman across the table from me.

She has so much to say, but doesn't quite know where I want to go with our interview, so she falls quiet and stares at me. I ask her the question that's been on my mind for awhile: what makes a Vermonter? (Or for that matter, what are the universal mechanics of claiming any regional identity? I hope that understanding her definition will help me understand those mechanics—a lofty goal of which she is completely unaware.)

"I think Vermonters are more self-reliant," she says, without identifying any group for comparison. "I think a lot of them are very quiet, or at least used to be. They work so hard. They get up real early in the morning, do their chores, then they work all day and go to bed early at night. I didn't do *that* part," she laughs.

This could be a fundamental part of regional pride just about anywhere—Wisconsin farmers, Sierra Nevada gold miners…Appalachian bootleggers… Self-reliance, modesty, hard work, these were once common virtues and are still highly regarded—something anyone would be proud to claim for themselves, and their definition of "us."

It's strange, and strangely heartening, to see such universal values in her definition of what makes Vermonters unique. I say it's heartening, because the more we recognize we have in common—especially in the descriptions we give of what we think sets us apart—the more hope there is for appreciating the essential humanity of others. Regional and individual identities are fantastic…but better still is when our differences are celebrated with the recognition of those things we also have in common.

I still can't quite explain what "Vermont" means as an adjective; what defines and differentiates a "Vermonter." I have a feeling, a sense, but it defies explanation. Perhaps Dot has the same problem.

She jokes about being a native who doesn't necessarily abide by her own stereotype, continuing "I can weed a garden just as well just before dark…I don't have to get up in the morning." Then before I can press her more about what makes a Vermonter, how she sees herself as an appropriate or inappropriate example of the type, she steers the conversation back to more concrete images and worldly concerns. I suspect she's buying time, and wonder in a fleeting moment how far it is ethical to direct a biographical interview away from where the subject wants to go. I relent, sit back, and enjoy the sweetness in her voice as she tells me more about herself.

"But you have to get up early in the morning to pick corn if you're going to go sell it," she concludes with the smile of someone who has transcended a minor hardship and can laugh about it now. She has never been big on mornings, even when she had to get up early for work, and still prefers to work well beyond the midnight hour and rise in time for lunch. While most of the working world is soundly asleep, Dot is wide awake and bustling around her home, smoking and reading and petting Nelly.

"And the freedom!" she continues, coming back around to my question. "The freedom in Vermont! I
210

mean, for me to live here where I can see everywhere and I can walk anywhere, and no one can stop me... that is worth...well, there's no money to buy it." We speak of Vermonters' love for the mountains, the views, the air and the pace of life, and of her own roots in the land—her days working it, and her parents and brother interred within it. She had a career in another town, and a marriage that took her far down south, but it is no surprise that she returned—home. It has that effect.

You may rightly call Vermonters stubborn, or stoic, which they see as virtues; those are terms Dot proudly claims for herself. Her family had a way of dauntlessly facing hard work, and they as much as anyone informed her impression of what it means to be a Vermonter. Her father toiled over bobbins in the fabric mill and her grandparents got working before the sun came up.

Other Vermonters worked ten and twelve hour shifts in the granite quarries, suffering lung disease and frequent mishaps to bring paychecks home to their families. Vermont's railroad men kept the steam locomotives chugging, laying and repairing tracks through White River Junction, Hartford, and beyond, with no health insurance to cover disabilities from disfiguring accidents that ended careers—that was the way of life across America in the early 1900s, graphically illustrated in local history. Dot grew up at the tail end of this hard epoch, and thrived. She worked on the farm while going to school, and when old enough to work in White River Junction, waited tables at the Polka Dot Diner.

"In high school, I was saving my money because I knew I was going to college," she explains. The Polka Dot was then, as it is now, just a few feet from the railroad tracks in the heart of White River Junction. White River Station is less than a block away, and from it came a steady stream of hungry travelers and rail crews. Plenty of characters we would now call "unsavory" or "rustically charming" frequented the lunch counter, and dealing with them took a certain skill set Dot quickly developed.

"Those people were tougher than nails, those waitresses," she recalls with zest. "Those railroad men came in all the time, and they (the waitresses) protected me like I was their daughter. They were so nice to me," as her voice softens, hardening again slightly. "If those railroad men would start getting wise, they'd come over and...(the men) wouldn't do it anymore! It taught me a lot about people," she says; dealing with that wide range of folks became an aspect of the work she saw as a benefit in and of itself, and one she cherished at later jobs as well.

The money she earned waiting tables helped her attend Posse, a girl's college near Boston that invited her to study on a basketball scholarship. She accepted readily, and set forth to live for the first time outside the realm of Hartford. Forged on the farm and tempered through sports and work at the Polka Dot, she was a product of Vermont as strong as anyone else who beat the Great Depression with their own two hands. Dot was ready to take on the world.

What she left behind was the Polka Dot diner in its heyday and a downtown, down-turning White River Junction that still had clothing and jewelry stores, supply shops and thrift stores, and two hotels that survived on business from the railroad...the sort of place that was making a stalwart, if faltering, go of things despite the

212

Great Depression's lingering effects. Those who lived in the villages worked at the mills or on the railroad, or in the associated businesses. Everyone else lived outside of the villages, on rural plots or family farms.

This was the Vermont she grew up knowing, where villages were surrounded by farms that supported the town, and were in turned supported by the money and goods from the villages. It was an economic model familiar across America, from New England vegetable gardens to the cornfields in the Midwest and cattle ranches down south. Her life changed dramatically when she left Hartford; so did America in the following decades. Her family tended the farm as always, with her father working at the Cone Mill and her mother working at Colodny's Department Store in White River Junction. Richard finished high school first, and like his sister, his life would never be the same after leaving the farm. Dot went south to school in Boston, and Richard went east to war in Europe.

He flew fighter planes over occupied territory, returning safely from fifty seven missions. "He would go out in a squadron, and they would peel off and go after the Germans and knock 'em," she boasts of her brother. "One thing he refused to do, they wanted him to go down on some civilians. He saw, one day, they were coming out of church. He wouldn't fire on 'em. He refused. He was up there high enough (in rank) then that they didn't say anything. Can you imagine? Even though Hitler was terrible, still, some of those people didn't deserve that, and he didn't do it." His strength of character—which I have the impression is a Howard family trait—overruled a direct order, which is anathema in the military. His wits kept him safe for fifty-seven sorties. And then he flew another one.

"Fifty eight, that was one too many," she explains. While Dot was playing basketball at Posse, Richard crash landed behind enemy lines and was taken prisoner. "He was always in a box, it's called, doing something wrong, out in the hot sun, 'cause he was always trying to escape," she gushes. Maybe it's an American thing that he was especially independent and stubborn; maybe it's a Vermont thing. After the American Revolution, Vermont remained an independent state for fourteen years; its citizens do things their own way, on their own time, and this one didn't much fancy that liberty being stripped away as a prisoner of war.

Richard's was certainly a family strength, the tough kind that raised his parents and grandparents out of bed before dawn every morning and sustained his female relations through graduation from high school and college when women weren't expected even to attend. The fine line between nature and nurture is hard to draw, especially in a case where they dovetail so well: a hardworking, stubborn family in a state renowned for the same. But in any event, he had heart, and strength beyond the muscles that dwindled after months of meager rations. It is said that uncommon courage was a common virtue in World War II, words that certainly apply to Richard.

When rescued by Allied forces, the proud former quarterback of Hartford High had outlived many of the other prisoners, some of the guards…and weighed only seventy-five pounds. "They wouldn't even let him come home," Dot says with a strange kind of pride. "They took him to the hospital until he put on some weight. He was a big man, and he went through hell. But he sure

214

did his mission!"

And he sure inspired Dot to believe in herself. When she moved away to college and a life on her own, she relied on her family's strength and her own stubbornness. During the school year she worked towards a degree in education, and during the summers she worked for money to get through the next year. A friend told her of an appealing place in Maine—a resort for the socially and financially elite. "You'd get board, room, and one day a week off," she said before adding "and I could learn about people! Ninety, ninety five percent of people were nice. Only the cook (wasn't). Beware the chefs!"

Dot put her people-skills to use, learning fast how to deal with the chefs. When a customer sends something back, "say, (they) ask for steak rare, and they send it back to be served well done, you know who the cook would yell at?" she asks with pepper on her words. "You know how I worked that one out? I threw it (out). When no one was looking…(I) put it through as a new order," and she shrugs her shoulders like a cunning schoolgirl getting away with something behind a teacher's back— which, in a way, she was. "How's that for thinking?" It served her well at home, and kept peace on the job.

Her first day was marred by an accident, though— one from which she recovered with customary aplomb. "You carry these big trays up here," she says, raising a hand instinctively up over her shoulder, "and they're full. When you came out the (kitchen) door, the people who owned it sat right by the door. Well, when I first tried it, guess where all the food went? On those people! But you know, they didn't yell at me much. I don't think they even yelled, they just picked it up. That was a good place." She worked there for three summers.

One of her greatest honors was waiting on Eleanor Roosevelt, who at the time was the First Lady of the United States and one of the most revered women in America. "I waited on Eleanor," she beams. "I did! She was nice, I talked to her." She was also deeply impressed by the woman, she says, and inspired; she had a special appreciation for Eleanor Roosevelt's strength and social consciousness, which she cites among the woman's many virtues. To Dot's delight, their paths would cross again many years later.

When the summers turned towards autumn she rode the train back south to Posse. At the time, Posse only granted three year degrees that were just shy of a full Bachelor's, so she enrolled at Temple University in Philadelphia to finish her degree on another basketball scholarship. She played on the starting rotation for their women's team despite only being there one year, and having never competed with them before—which is unheard of in college sports, but just the way it happened with Dot.

With her degree in hand, with her courage and character, empathy and an honest love of people—and her grandmother's example in valuing education—she felt called to be a public school teacher.

But she missed her summer job. "I've always loved Maine anyway," she says, talking about the coast and how she enjoys the ocean. As much as she appreciates Maine's beauty, though, and much as she misses the scenery, "I wouldn't want to live there," she continues. "I like Vermont better." She smiles, saying no more, folding her hands on the table. Home is, after all, where the heart is.

She returned directly to Vermont with her degree

216

and ambitions to teach, and visited an old contact in a very important position. The Hartford High School principal "had a chance to go to Bellows Falls," she says, introducing him as a friend—one she made years before as a student. "He called me and said 'Dot, I'm going to Bellows Falls, would you like to go in with me?' So see, I knew him four years before I even got there! I didn't even apply for a job!" She accepted his invitation, showed up, and became their new gymnastics instructor and coach. Reputation matters in small towns, and the one she earned as a student set up her career as a teacher.

* * * * *

The town of Bellows Falls, Vermont, is forty-two miles south of Hartford Village, and, she said, quite similar. Each is a small mountain hamlet with certain family names going back beyond memory, but Dot's observations are keener than mine. "I didn't find it any different," she says. "It was a small Vermont town. And of course, their big bent was the mill, and the electric company. The people were rich and poor, like all places. But they were friendly. I got along well with all of them. It was sorta like living here (in Hartford).

"White River Junction, Bellows Falls, Hartford Village," she muses, "no, Bellows Falls was too small. But not much different from White River." Though she was new, the town felt familiar. "I was used to living in a small town, where everybody else knew your business. Which they do! You have to live in a city if you don't want anyone else to know your business. Besides, what did I care? I didn't steal anything.

"I coached basketball, softball, tennis, and field hockey," she continues. When she started, she only really knew how to play basketball; the rest she learned along the way, the same as how she picked up other skill sets everywhere she worked. "I learned all that. All we had was basketball in high school, college. I learned very quickly how to play field hockey," and the other sports so she could make them available to girls in Bellows Falls.

Basketball took her out of the Upper Valley to tournaments around New England, and got her into a college she could not otherwise afford; Dot wanted such opportunities for her students as well. "I wanted them to have those sports," she says, "so I did it. I didn't get paid, you know, for a long time. I'd go to that school board, and keep…" She trails off, eyes set and locked somewhere between old frustration and a rebel's gleam.

"Things weren't like they are today," she continued with a slightly softer tone, "with women's rights and all. But that's one thing I liked at Bellows Falls, they expected to see a women's basketball team." Her voice resonates now with pride; pride on behalf of the town more than herself, for their accommodation was ahead of the times. "I got equal time in the gym, which was unheard of in those days. And they followed those games." The town's support was somewhat novel; few people, beyond those playing, followed women's sports in the 1940s. Though the stands were rarely as full for the women's games as for the men's games, support from the players' families and the community at large reassured Dot that she was on the right track.

After school she coached a "town team," as she described them—basketball players who competed in
218

their own league. The players were high school kids and adults, and under Dot's instruction and encouragement they rose to win the New England championship. For their success, they were invited to St. Joseph, Missouri, farther west than Dot had ever traveled before. "They gave all of us time off, and uniforms," and practice facilities to get ready, she explains. The school supported the team, and the town rallied behind their champions, sending them westward to represent rural Vermont against the best teams in the country. "Imagine them giving all of us time off and letting us use the school uniforms and basketball..." she leads.

"Imagine playing the best team in the United States...from Vermont!" They played that team first, and lost badly—69 to 3, their only points coming from free throws. "And they were so discouraged!" she blurts, tapping the table with her left hand; there is unfaltering pride in her eyes. "We played one more game and did much better in that one. I said 'look at it, you saw Niagara Falls, you had a wonderful trip... what's so bad about that?'" And on the way back they had a true Midwest adventure: outrunning a tornado— she tells me that story with her mischievous eyes ablaze.

"I was driving one car, and we literally outran that tornado out there," she explains as if she got back just yesterday. "They have awful ones out there. That sky was so black...I said 'we really have to go fast!' We did outrun it! That was very frightening!" Though frightening, she tells the story—at least through memory's amber lens—like a great adventure.

Basketball made it happen—that trip, those adventures, the opportunities for Dot and her team— but not alone; it took Dot's commitment to sports, to working with people, and developing something she loves to keep a recreational team of Vermonters at the top of their game and lead them halfway across the continent back when such travel was exceedingly rare.

This was her professional life in the forties and fifties, the face she showed Bellows Falls from the sidelines and in the newspaper. During the summers she left Vermont, traveling south for a personal life she could only have on a Marine Corps airbase in North Carolina. "My ex-husband was a pilot there," she recounts respectfully, but not energetically. They had met in Hartford years before. "I went with him all through high school. I had college and was teaching, so he would come on leave. He got plenty of leave, so we'd meet in New York. I saw more plays than I'll ever see again in my lifetime," she says with raillery, and yet, with a certain goodhearted nostalgia—such is the careful balance she walks, between alacrity and acerbity. It feels familiar, and yet specific—perhaps only in how well it fits her personality.

When the summer vacations began, she rode the train south out of Vermont to live for a few months as the wife of Lieutenant Bradley Jones. While her professional life was back north in Bellows Falls, and her heart farther north still, near Hartford, her marriage drew her to the base—where her disdain for military life kept her on edge. Though her brother was a decorated career military officer, by then already high in the ranks of the Army Air Corps (which became the US Air Force in 1947), she never developed a taste for the military.

"I hated it," are her exact words. "In the first place, I didn't like it, and I'll say that a thousand times. When I went to church on the Marine base, this major's wife got a hold of me—Brad was a lieutenant—and said 'you can't talk,' I was laughing and joking with anybody I knew, 'you are not allowed to talk to an enlisted man.'" Now her scorn comes through unfiltered.

"That's not the way I was brought up, I couldn't do that." As a people-person, she bristled at what she saw as an arbitrary division of social life into elite and common—and resented that anyone would attempt to dictate how and to whom she could be friendly. Her upbringing told her what was right—and that snootily avoiding certain people only because of rank was wrong. Her independence welled behind her social grace, souring her further on military life.

She and Brad were well cared for; they often stayed at the homes of officers who were deployed elsewhere for long periods of time, and Brad's duties included managing the officer's club. Still, the life of a military wife—if even for only few weeks out of the year—did not satisfy Dot Jones. "He'd be gone, sometimes for three or four days," she says, "and I thought 'well what am I doing here?' Fourteen years of that was enough."

Their marriage turned upon her father's death. Her mother and grandmother were living in the homestead, and she felt drawn back home more than ever. "When my father was dead," she says, tobacco smoke curling along the ceiling, "I didn't want to go (south anymore); I didn't want to be down there, I wanted to be up here." Lorna crushes out a cigarette in the other room and adds "I think that's a typical thing for a Vermonter."

"I wanted to be up here," Dot repeats, "so, that was that, and it was very amiable. But that was fourteen years." Brad remained in North Carolina, and Dot began spending her summers and holidays back on the

221

homestead. Her routine already found her home most weekends, making the commute from Bellows Falls north on Eisenhower's interstate among the trucks that usurped the railway business.

The barn where she discovered basketball was gone—torn down at her late father's behest, the wood given to war veterans so they could build homes. With the passing of her grandfather, and then her father, the farm slowed down until there were no more chickens or pigs, no more vast tracts of cultivated land, and what remained of the livestock and gardens were what her mother and grandmother could manage.

Other family farms in their White River Valley were sold, or slowed their production as successive generations took jobs in town or on other farms. The Great Depression had ended decades before, but with the drop off in rail business and America's cultural swing towards urbanization, the small village town was still having troubles. Dot's life changed while she was away, and so too had the farm and villages and era she left behind—but none were done changing yet.

For twenty years she coached sports, starting with pre-season practices and ending with championship seasons that ran up to graduation time. The hours were long, but she made no complaint to me, and likely, any complaints she voiced then were raised in the quiet privacy Vermonters prefer. Through high school sports she met another teacher and coach—Lorna—with whom she developed a lasting acquaintance. "We became friends through basketball," Dot explains, glancing into the other room at Lorna as she sits smoking near a window, smiling. "It's good to have a friend around." Lorna taught in Chester, Vermont, where one day

222

Eleanor Roosevelt was scheduled to make a public appearance.

"I said to the teachers 'let's put (the students) in the car and drive up, who gets to see Eleanor Roosevelt?'" Dot straightens in her chair and gives a Cheshire grin. "So we did, without asking!" That would, with its rebellious lack of authorization and waivers and permission slips, never happen today…and the gleam in her eye suggests it probably shouldn't have happened back then. But she made it happen and got away with it, all in the name of seeing one of her role models. Her respect for Eleanor, the cultural leader and champion for the rights of the underprivileged, makes perfect sense.

Eleanor was the earliest First Lady to direct the attention she received as the President's wife, towards agitating for social action. She was revered for her strength of character, her confidence, and her empathetic way of dealing with a great diversity of people— attributes I find in Dot, which helped her as a waitress and throughout her career in education. Also like Dot, Eleanor was a proud athlete of some renown—she was an archer, and a Rompala Buck she shot hung in her husband's Presidential Library—who retained her social capital as a lady, in a time when women's athletics were considered cute at best…and certainly not serious. Nine years after Eleanor published an article on shooting that buck, in doing so breaking several taboos about "ladylike" behavior and a woman's role in society, Dot began her struggle against the status quo to legitimize and expand women's high school athletics.

In their own ways, the public figure and the school teacher each worked to advance the rights of people by advancing the rights of women…and insisting on equal public respect. It might seem audacious to draw parallels between them, one who was nominated for a posthumous Nobel Peace Prize and the other, a school teacher from a rural town, but similarities exist that help illustrate the admiration and respect Dot felt for the First Lady…and why Dot kidnapped her students to hear Eleanor speak.

Dot's immediate reaction was to pack the kids under her watch into a car and share the experience with everyone, as she describes the day as being one of the rare *act now or forever regret not doing it* experiences we are occasionally presented with. The children enjoyed it, she claims, adding how such a spur of the moment act could cost a teacher her job these days; there again, Dot's initiative and bold personality led the way…and there again, she does not regret it.

* * * * *

Bellows Falls supported their women's teams for the twenty years she coached them…for which she is very thankful. "I was lucky," she says. "I loved it in Bellows Falls, they were good to me. I appreciated that. …They were working class people, they supported sports… for the girls even!" But twenty years of coaching and teaching gym class left her hungry for something new, a novel way to reach her students. To put it succinctly, as Dot is want to do, "I wanted to stop being a coach because twenty years is a long time."

She was a little more restless than she lets on… and yearning for a new challenge. Dot took courses from Keene State with several other teachers, earning her Master's degree in guidance. "See, guidance in the elementary school was comparatively new," she explains. "I loved the coaching and all that, but after awhile…"

By then the principal she followed to Bellows Falls had become the district's superintendent, and change was in the air. The athletic conference recognized her contributions to women's athletics, especially how she began new women's teams in previously male-exclusive sports, built public support for women's athletics, and worked individually with girls who used sports to get into college. They showed their appreciation by naming their conference the "Dot Jones League," which encompassed all women's sports and bore her name for forty years. Meanwhile, Dot rose to the challenge of a new vocation: guidance counselor, where she could be a leader and role model in different ways.

She served five elementary schools, dealing with cases of truancy and problem behavior, counseling at-risk children before anyone used the term "at-risk," or responded by drugging children with psychotropic medication. Where there was a problem, there was Dot, and she faced the new realm of "guidance counseling" with her intuition and sense of justice. "I had to take the lunchroom one time," she relates, "and a boy threw apple sauce in another boy's face. The other boy didn't have any...but I did! The boy was cryin', the other kid was yellin', and I went over and threw it in his face! And he got up and ran home! I called his mother and she said, 'cause she had me in school, 'I know Dot if you did that, he deserved it.' I'd hate to try that today!"

She answered truancy calls as well, looking in on children who failed to show up for school without explanation, and she wasn't afraid to address the matter straightaway with whomever she encountered. "I had appointments with (some) of these people, you know," she says, "but not all of 'em, 'cause they didn't want to see guidance counselors. I went into one (home)…and the mother and father were having sex! Not in the other room, right there in front of the kid, and I'm right there in front of them! I really reamed them out. I just thought that was so bad, not that they were having sex, but in front of their kid, and company."

She could write a book on strange experiences as a guidance counselor—including anecdotes like the time she helped a mother chase her third grade son as he ran naked out of his house and amok through the neighborhood… Common through all of her stories, from the girl she found in a home sitting next to her dead mother to the children in even more bizarre and tragic circumstances, is the idea that she truly cared for those in her charge. What began with her mother's urging—and her desire—to go to school with many and different children grew into her love of people.

The skills she developed in dealing with tough railroad men and high society alike put her in good stead for the wide cross section of society with whom she dealt as a counselor. Underneath it all was her confidence that she could help those who needed someone, and that feistiness born of growing up as a little sister on a rural farm. As we are the sums of our experiences and perceptions, Dot Jones is forty years of educational leadership and experience in the spry body of an eighty-five year old Vermonter.

She keeps a few mementos handy, totems from her teaching days; a few important ones are out of the way on the china cabinet, but handy all the same. One is a poem written by Jennifer Stowell, a girl Dot coached. "During the quarter century in B.F. Town / Girl's sports did climb to a place of reknown [sic] / Many a team tasted the fruit of victory / Due to her coaching and fine comradie [sic]," the poem reads in part. Jennifer is but one of thousands of children Dot coached and guided over the years.

With her friends bidding her a fond farewell from Bellows Falls, and Lorna's support, Dot moved her life north—back home, to her roots, and her elderly mother on the farm where both of them had been raised. Doris Mock needed her daughter, "even though she was very independent," Dot explains.

"She belonged to all the organizations, the World War Mothers, high up in the American Legion Auxiliary...see where I get it from?" Indeed—hard work and service themes run deep through her brother's military career, her mother's volunteerism, and her own work in the schools. For all the personal reasons Dot moved home from Bellows Falls, though, taking care of her mother was perhaps the strongest.

"I wanted her to be comfortable here," she says, warmly. "I wanted to make sure that everything could be done. Still have a big garden, can vegetables, do all those things, and we did. We could eat; we did not have to buy food, that's what we did. She was always running off to work, leaving me directions 'when this boils so many minutes, you take and tighten the jar and...' I forgot what, but I was always left with some little chore in canning. She made a lot of pickles, a lot of tomatoes. I swear, we could live without..." Her mother worked at the five and dime store in White River Junction for fifty years, and tended the farm until her very last days.

The women kept the family's farming legacy alive, if only insomuch as producing what they alone needed. Complacency is just not a part of the Howard family.

The village Dot returned to had changed dramatically. Rail traffic had dwindled to a fraction of its former bustle, and the Polka Dot no longer teemed with railroad men and travelers. "It used to be filled all the time, (the trains) were coming in and out," she says. When Vermont passed the state sales tax, most of the businesses either folded or moved east, across the river to New Hampshire—as Larry Chase lamented.

Dot observes, "All the ones there (in White River Junction) couldn't make a living. I couldn't believe it, there were no more stores. When you came to town, there was nothing, hardly, you know, except the Hotel Coolidge." The thought darkens her face, and she looks down at the table, then back up to meet my gaze.

Her family farm, like the empty Twin State Fruit Company building falling in on itself along Railroad Row, had become somewhat anachronistic. The change from the family farms of her childhood to the large company farms was nearly complete, though many old farm families maintained large gardens out of pride and habit. Dot bought her milk and eggs in town rather than going to the barn after them—there wasn't a barn anymore, just a small red shed used for storage. The area, the people, and the times had changed, presenting new opportunities to the younger generations and changing what the others once took for granted. But there were still opportunities in town, chances for community involvement that she couldn't resist—Dot is not the kind of woman to fade quietly into the Green Mountains, canning tomatoes. Not by a long shot.

She canned, certainly, and she planted large sweet corn and squash gardens, but she also jumped headfirst into community service for "something to do," she explains. "I belonged to…a women's club, (was a) board member of the Hartford Library. President of the Historical Society…to keep busy. And to get with people. I didn't want to just hibernate somewhere, and I wanted a purpose in doing it, I didn't want to just go out and mingle. I'm interested in the Historical Society, definitely." Her most adventurous move was running for Town Lister, an elected position, in the hometown where she had not lived in forty years.

Lorna observes that the Howard/Mock family names still held quite a lot of esteem in the area at the time—Richard was the head of both the Vermont National Guard and the Vermont Air Guard, and Bob Howard was a locally known millionaire inventor and businessman. "When…she decided to campaign for Lister," Lorna explains, "(she) found out that there were a lot of people who remembered (her) that (she) didn't even remember, possibly because of (her) last name." Dot held the job for as long as she cared to hold it—more than a decade and a half.

"I was sixteen years the Lister at the Town of Hartford," she says with pride, showing me a resolution from the Town of Hartford Board of Selectmen that gives her "A vote of appreciation for her seventeen years of outstanding service." The odd year comes from her tenure as president of the Hartford Historical Society, a position that she has filled for quite a while now—the seventeen year figure is a bit shy of her actual accomplishment, but you won't find Dot complaining. Nor would you have found Dot at the Town Meeting where she was honored!

She explains, "When I retired as a Lister, they gave a big speech at the Town Meeting. Everybody started clapping, guess what: I wasn't there. They got the surprise, I probably wasn't awake!" Her smile is sly and cunning, and wild enough to be endearing. "My hours aren't (like those kept by) other normal folk," she reiterates. Nor has her life followed traditional paths, except perhaps in her values.

These values, of family, independence, self reliance and a strong sense of home, are common between the Howard and the Mock families...and have brought them home to Hartford for generations. "We always had a close family," Dot says, recalling her youth when three generations lived together in this home. Lorna adds from her reclining chair how one Christmas there were eighteen people gathered around the tree in the living room, eating food grown out back and cherishing their time together.

"We always had someone play Santa Claus," Dot recalls. "My brother and I, we always believed in Santa Claus. One time it was a warm Christmas, we sat outdoors and said 'how much longer should we decide we believe in Santa?'" She's the kind of woman who still, in her eighties, wants to believe in Santa Claus. "It was so much fun, and they'd ring a bell when Santa was coming, and we'd go upstairs and listen to him, and then they'd say 'OK, you can come down now.'"

There was a hole in the floor of Richard's room where an old stovepipe used to come through, and they would lie on their stomachs and watch their uncles play cards below. Did they ever spy on Santa through that hole? "I'd never tell," she says with a wily grin.

She returned home frequently during her time in Bellows Falls, and other family members visited often as well. The home provided a vacation spot, a connection to the family, and a relaxing, concrete tie to the rural Vermont they left behind for lives outside the Green Mountains. Richard and his son visited the farm yearly while playing in a golf tournament nearby, on a course he used to play with his sister. "My nephew is still playing in the big one they have at Dartmouth, this tournament," she explains. "He played with his father while he was alive, it was a big deal. They'd come back here to tell me how they were gonna win it!" she says with a melancholy-turning smile. "Well, they didn't." Richard passed away awhile ago.

Bob Howard "came up last summer," she says, further illustrating how the farm is a pilgrimage site in her family. "He stayed here; he wanted to renew his ties and so on." There was always space for family, from the six bedrooms to the couches and floors. They all filled up during holidays, though the last decade has seen a precipitous decrease in cheerful traffic. Family was "always coming up to live. I guess because the farm was a good environment, maybe they were getting in trouble or something. …They all came back on vacation. I knew that we were going to have three, four, five extra people every night. I didn't mind." After all, having house guests can be a real help sometimes.

"They'd go fishing and catch more trout, and then go back out again!" she says. She doesn't like trout, she adds, but she loves the memory, and the way these stories make this place a home.

Cousins and guests came from all over the country, all drawn to the rural serenity and the locus of family history. "One of 'em went to school here for a year," she adds. "Then my other uncle, Harold Howard, he was more than a Lieutenant Colonel in the Army. His girls have lived all over the world, 'cause they always went wherever he was sent. My aunt Florence is ninety, and her husband...they lived here, five, six, seven of 'em, 'til she got an apartment. But she didn't want one while the war was going on, because she might be able to go with him, so she lived here."

Family members don't return as frequently anymore, Richard having passed away and the children of children growing ever more distant from the homestead—but the ties that bind are fastened securely to Dot's heart, and her memories are fond. People and places each shape our lives, and this home knits them together for Dot. What makes a Vermonter? Their family ties, and their family's ties to the land, in no small parts.

And so Dot falls quiet, thinking about my question again—what makes a Vermonter? She stands, smiling down at Nelly. Lorna has left to run an errand, one last wisp of smoke rising from the ashtray by her empty chair in the living room. Even standing, Dot is barely taller than me as I sit here, quietly regarding this woman I admire.

The Howard and Mock families packed a lot of people into this old house; Dot has lived so much life in her one small body. She pulls her grey sweater even across her shoulders and walks to the window, looking out over the White River a few dozen yards away, as if by turning away from me she closes a door to the past and moves into one perfect late afternoon moment.

Though she stands just feet away, I hear her as if from somewhere else. "What else is there, how much more is there to say?"

Joe Pogar—Legally blind and almost completely deaf at 98, he still plays his fiddle remarkably well. Pictured here, he has just put the instrument down and is transitioning from his performance—for an audience only he could see—back to the present moment.

Joe Pogar
The Older the Fiddle, the Sweeter the Music

You have a length of wood, three inches a side and three feet long, any tools you like and as much time as you want. With that piece of wood, what would you make?

Joe Pogar's hands are small, and strong under the loose skin you expect on hands that have not stopped working in nearly a century. Growing up in Granville, New York, Joe found himself with just such a piece of wood in his hands, a jackknife in his pocket, and inspiration from a Boy Scout manual. He carved a wooden chain with more than a dozen links, and upon one end he made a small cage with a captive ball that rolls around inside. The links, the ball, and the ornaments on each end of the chain have never been disconnected—all were fashioned where they are, carved by hand from a solid piece of wood. "All I had was a knife," he tells me this winter morning as we sit around the wood stove in the kitchen of his home in Wilder, Vermont, just uphill from White River Junction.

"I would carve a link, and make sure I didn't cut the next link." He stretches the chain between his hands, pulling it straight and letting it sag with soft wooden clinks. "Boy, it was a job. I had plenty of time back then." The chain hangs over his wood stove, underlining a small mantle with mugs, knickknacks, and a small builder's square. His kitchen is cozy, but the three of us here today fit comfortably around a kitchen table. The room is just large enough for two cabinets, an electric stove and a large sink, hanging dish cabinets, two countertops and a refrigerator—many of which he built himself. And there is the wood stove, next to which he spends much of his time in the winter, warming his right knee.

"A wood fire is good heat," he explains, blue eyes staring six inches to my left, smiling nervously. This is our first morning together, our first interview; the open question hangs silently in the air, of whether I'll need or want to come back again—whether this is Joe's only chance to tell his story to a stranger, or his first meeting with a friend. You tell different things to friends, than strangers; you tell different stories when you know you have only one chance to tell them. The question, silently hanging, can be answered only by time.

I have come to hear stories from Hartford's past, to learn more about White River Junction from a man who lived through eras I can't visit. But also I've come to meet a man who has lived nearly a century, more than four times longer than I have, to see what he can teach me about life. That is a pretty heady goal, but then, I have learned a lot from several enjoyable visits with other elderly Vermonters. I am at ease, and have high hopes.

Across the table sits his best friend and neighbor, Winona Hary. Twenty some-odd years his junior, she has a spark that seems positively youthful. They play music together in his living room, Joe on the fiddle, Winona on the ancient upright piano with sheet music so heavily notated it effectively holds two songs per page—one in print, one in notes. She sits across the table from the stove, a grey wool sweater spread over her lap.

"I have hot water heat here," Joe continues, "but it's not like a wood fire. It's steady, but it doesn't penetrate. I have arthritis in my knee, and I put it over here," he says, tapping his right foot on the floor near the stove's black iron door. The stove is just large enough to heat the kitchen, just large enough to cook upon if one is really intent to cook upon wood heat, and fits perfectly into the décor: half-panel walls, small wooden lamps, and cabinets everywhere. Across the table, atop a cabinet, is one of Joe's "pump handle lamps," which he made in his basement workshop years ago; when you depress the handle on the miniature water pump, it pulls a chain and turns on the lamp.

"I buy (firewood) split," he explains, rubbing his hands together over the stove—they are strong, but no longer suited for axe handles and work gloves. "Next month, if I can, I'll get two, three cords, and season it, let it dry for next year. It'll be dry then. Then I'll put it over here, and get more for the next year, for the next ten years!"

He likely won't see the end of another decade's supply, but he doesn't seem troubled by this, and talks of the future he might see in terms that suggest he expects he will...but won't be troubled if he doesn't. "Well, I think, probably, when time comes, the old ticker will stop and that'll be it," he tells me rather abruptly, as if reading my mind—or perhaps, to keep me from blundering into the question on my own. This comfort with the certainty of death (which is certain for everyone), and his acceptance of the uncertainty of when, is quite striking—he seems almost glib.

Perhaps it is his way of dealing with the vagary; I hope to have as much aplomb in seventy years. "I hope it's not a long-term thing," he continues. "But I, see, I've been retired thirty-three years. The government probably wishes I'd go!"

He uses humor as a shield; I also use humor to dull sharp edges and assuage my fears. So do a lot of people—it works. This acceptance of his age, the past and the vagaries of the future—with genuine wit about it all—is part of Joe's affecting charm.

The firewood he speaks of comes in by truck—sometimes his own, when Winona fills the bed of Joe's El Camino pickup. That twenty-nine year old vehicle has a V8 engine, chrome fenders, and a carburetor, and was built back in the days before disposable living trends brought us cars that only last a few years. He nods towards the garage beside his home and tells me about his truck, making that connection between firewood and his El Camino on his own. Then he says he remembers when horses still outnumbered cars.

"Cars were slow then!" Winona adds emphatically, looking at Joe as if to coax him into telling me something I would never read in the history books—something only he could know.

"That's like the Vermonter," he says, "who invited a Texas rancher to come up, and the rancher said 'how big of a spread do you got?' He said 'oh, about two hundred acres.' Well the Texan said 'that's a piddly amount. Back home I've got a ranch, I get in my car at one end of my ranch and it takes me all day to get to the other.' The old Vermonter said 'I had a car like that one time too.'"

Winona knows Joe's guileless charm well—he

238

is a kind man, and a good friend. They met six years ago, and rely on each other for the sort of help and companionship that means so much when life quietly closes up around you. Widowed in 1997 upon the death of her husband, Louis, she came to live on Passumpsic Avenue in 2000; Joe lives right next door.

"I had met Joe once before," she explains. "When I moved in, someone mentioned that he needed help, so I said 'well I can do that.'" They've been good friends ever since, and enjoy regular lunches together at the Bugbee Senior Center or out on the town in White River Junction. She drives, he directs, and the widow and widower help each other through their golden years.

"Hey Nona," Joe says with a grin so wide his hair perks up. "Let's play for him 'Goofus!'" She agrees, adding that it's a splendid idea, and hurries to clear the way into the living room. "I've played violin my whole life, Dave," he says, standing with a spring in his step. He explains on our way to the living room that he began playing when he was seven, at his father Szymon's insistence.

"They had gypsies that would go around, and play violin," he explains. These gypsies wandered around Poland, and his father liked their music, which I presume is why Szymon encouraged his son to play the fiddle—perhaps it comforted the man. It definitely changed Joe's life. He grew up listening to very little music at all, and it was not until he was thirteen that he heard a radio. As he picks his fiddle out of a black, fur lined case, he tells me about listening that first time to a "boxing match between Jack Dempsey and Luis Firpo. Dempsey won." And then, smiling towards the piano, he raises his bowstring and says "Ready Nona?"

239

She smiles and says yes, and they take off together through a long and winding melody. His violin leads the way while she keeps the beat playing chords. These plaster walls glow from decades of homespun music played right here in the living room; the scene is comfortable, with a sense of antiquity, from the faded blue easy chair to the antique tables and handmade wooden trim around the walls. Everything about this room is old, time tested, from the faintly out of tune piano to the slightly sharp violin and the smell of cats—specifically, "Miss Kitty," a grey cat with a bobbed tail that visited Joe several years ago and decided to stay. Miss Kitty aside, these things around the room—right down to the dust in the corners—have soaked up Joe's fiddle music for decades.

There is a bumper sticker on his truck that proclaims, "The older the fiddle, the sweeter the music." It's right, though a few adjustments would tame the instrument's shrillest highs. Joe can play by memory and feel, but tuning is a bit more challenging. Winona's shoulders bounce slightly on off-beats under the old grey sweater she wrapped around herself. This room is much cooler than the kitchen, but not uncomfortable. Joe sways with his music, bobbing and weaving his head to the rhythm of quarter notes and a lifetime of memories. They bear down on the last beat and shout in chorus "Goofus!" Winona turns her sheet music while Joe introduces the next tune—another one he is ready to perform purely from memory.

"When we play, we have a little spiel," he says. "Back when I was a youngster, there were very few cars on the road. The roads were dirt roads, and a lot of horses, and there were mules. Big ears. Now we're gonna play 'Flop Eared Mule,'" and he trails off into the opening notes. The song is old, older than Joe, with sounds straight out of a speakeasy or dance at a barn raising. He remembers plenty of both with a mind as sharp as the high B's from his fiddle. These are the songs of the early twentieth century, the northeastern mountain music and lively folksongs that invoke a time gone by. The living room is crowded with old chairs and heavy wooden tables, knickknacks from a lifetime of harmless fads, and upholstery from several fashions ago, the music swirling between it all and bringing to life the spaces in between until the room is alive with nostalgia. If you fall asleep in a moment like this, could you wake up in another era?

This is the fourth home I have visited in meeting Vermonters, and the fourth in which I have been welcomed with a hearty smile—and a bit of initial wariness. Joe's house is warm and comfortable, showing rich history written in cracks and nicks by children from several generations. The wood stove reminds me of the one near Dot's kitchen table, or the one in Harold's home. The tidiness of the clutter suggests an active man, too involved to put things away, too neat to let them lie about haphazardly.

There are paintings on the wall, photographs on shelves, and an almost palpable sense of rural America. Specifically, in the natural wood, the smells, the warmth of the stove and the mix of barn wood frames and a glowing neon violin-shaped clock on the wall, I find a balance of the country, the city, the old and the new. Joe is not a relic of an age gone by, nor does he try to be anything he is not; Joe is simply Joe, and tells stories from ten decades as easily as I talk about today's weather. That's part of the timeless charm that pours through his fiddle and over the room, as thick and rich as the last notes he plays on the old violin.

And now the song is over, and we amble back into the kitchen, to the stove, where Joe props his knee in front of the iron door. He points out the lamps again. "You've got this one here, a swing lamp," he says, talking about the lamp mounted to the wall overhead. It articulates on two wooden arms—swing it out and you can position the lamp in a wide arc. "It's good to have over the bed, if you're reading at night." He reaches up and touches it as if he can see exactly where it is, which he can't—Joe has been blind for several years, and would be completely deaf without his custom hearing aid.

That is why he plays everything from memory now.

That is why most of the tools downstairs are gone, and why someone cut the power cord on his table saw.

That is why Winona Hary sits quietly across the kitchen table, repeating some of my questions loud enough for him to hear.

And that is why he no longer plays with the Dartmouth Symphony or the Jolly Seniors, a group that toured hospitals and nursing homes playing familiar music to those in want of comfort. He lost his vision, as he puts it, in 1993, his ears being on a precipitous decline even then. But his memory is unaffected, for which he is grateful. Eighty years of practice ring sharply in his mind, and he can feel the notes in the quivering strings. The music takes him back to places long gone, among people who have slipped quietly into history. There in his living room he plays violin with Winona, but for those friends who passed and the good times they

242

shared. When he plays with his eyes closed he enters a timeless, sacred place full of anachronisms and music, friendly faces and beer and chicken and living rooms, his friends and his father each at their merriest. And, he plays because he likes it—he always has.

His hands have produced more than music—Joe is an expert craftsman. Glance anywhere in his home and you will see at least two things Joe made: cabinets and paintings, tables and beautiful stencil work on the plaster walls…and this entire kitchen, which Joe and his son built themselves. He picked up music, carpentry, cooking, finance, etc, through hard work and ingenuity.

Szymon only had basic tools, not like the many different types Joe kept in his Wilder home for so many years, but his father had something else that inspired and empowered Joe: drive and determination. "He had a saw," Joe says. "He'd use the saw to saw wood. He'd work all day, then come home and saw wood." Joe worked all day, then played music, worked with his hands, and picked up other skills. Working hard and keeping busy don't strike him as particularly noble attributes—he just did, because that is how one learns, and those are the sorts of things the men around him did.

They built furniture, worked on cars, and fixed things so they didn't have to suffer the cost—or embarrassment—of hiring someone to do for them what they felt were their own responsibilities. When Joe moved to White River Junction, he started with almost no possessions—but he valued hard work and dedication, and he learned things quite readily. These tools are much more valuable than hammers and saws.

His life in White River Junction began in a tent at a

work camp. Eventually he purchased and remodeled a house, furnishing and finishing it with his own hands, and filled it with his music and a large family. This home and the music in his living room are as much parts of Joe as his wispy gray hair and sun-marked skin; each line on his face holds a story like the grooves on a wax cylinder. He saw life as a blank piece of wood from which he could fashion just about anything, and everything he's made from life and lumber is a reflection of the man. As I came to know this house through his stories, I came to know Joe Pogar—an inspiring man with a wealth of history and perspective.

Perhaps knowing Joe won't change anyone's life, though it did for his wife Katherine Paul and his friend Winona; but perhaps in an increasingly disposable, insular world—we know more about Afghani politics than about our neighbors—what we need is to connect with people, like Joe, over coffee on a slow Vermont morning. Conversations like these comfort the mind and steady the nerves—seeing a man who has surely *been there* and *done that*, been through the good and bad and ugly in life, sitting there smiling so contentedly...just feels nice. If it truly is good to laugh, and good to hope, then it is good to know people like Joe.

* * * * *

That is how I met Joe. Now he welcomes me into his home every month, and we drink coffee and beer and talk about baseball and music. I don't like talking about baseball, but I like talking to Joe, and so we chat until it's time for him to bustle off to an appointment or run an errand with Winona. His life story began in 1908, and still feels far from over. As I came to know Joe, I came to see both how a man can build a life, and how a life can build a man. When he told me about that life, he began with his father.

Szymon Pogar emigrated from Poland to New York in 1905, where in a pub he met an American woman named Mary Billow. They were married that same year, and in 1908 made room for Josephus Pogar in their Granville, New York, home. "I keep tellin' people it's June 31st," Joe says of his birthday. "But they don't believe me."

"Why not?"

"Because there is no June 31st!" Winona chimes, slinging the punch line on Joe's joke. They make a good team.

"You know, I had a neighbor that since moved away. She called me up, wishing me a happy birthday. I told her 'Louise, no it isn't.' 'Well when is it?' 'September 31st.' 'Oh,' she said, 'I'll have to write that down.' About five minutes later she came over and said 'there is no September 31st!' I told her she's looking at the wrong calendar, it's the Julian Calendar, not the Gregorian!" Joe's real birthday is July 24th.

Szymon came to America with the coins in his pocket and built a life from scratch—establishing himself, working, marrying Mary and raising Joe and another son: John, five years younger and no longer with us. His inspiration to take that open future and make of it what he needed was perhaps the greatest legacy he gave his sons. As a teenager, Joe dropped out of high school to go to work, and never went back—life became his classroom.

"I self-educated myself to a certain degree," he

explains, "to a degree I don't have. I tell ya, if I'd gone to school to further my education, I'd'a been worse off, I don't know. I wouldn't be over here, probably! God knows where…"

Joe earned some money in those days playing violin, his first gigs coming from the American Legion when he was fifteen years old.

"There was no theater, and I played in the pit," he explains. "It wasn't classical, it was 'Happy Days (are Here Again).' It kind of changed the way I thought about music." Previously self-taught in classical music, that gig engaged him in a lifelong passion…one that really got humming in the secret back rooms at speakeasies. "In the summertime I played in the Adirondacks," he says, "at Scroom Lake. That was during Prohibition." he played backroom bars all through the mountains. "I'd leave about five o'clock in the evening, and wouldn't get home until five o'clock in the morning. We played until one, two o'clock," and then rode home over narrow, winding mountain roads. He developed a taste for show business, even rubbing shoulders with the famous songwriter W.C. Handy.

"Back in those days," he said, "the hotels, like in Chicago the Black Hawk, and New Jersey's Meadowlion, Pennsylvania Hotel, they all had dinner music, big bands. You've probably heard W.C. Handy, haven't you? He wrote the 'St. Louis Blues.' After that, I was around twenty years old, and there was a band from White Hall, New York. He came down and wanted me to play with 'em!"

This seems like a big break, a chance to validate any dreams he held of being a professional musician—but even the professionals struggle to work steadily. Despite his love for music, and his improving skills with fiddles, pianos, and other instruments, he saw the value of stable employment. He found it with the government: the Citizen's Conservation Corps welcomed him in 1935 as a field cook supporting their various civil service projects.

The CCC brought him to White River Junction, Vermont, in 1936 to feed the men working on the new Veteran's Affairs Hospital along Route 5. He slept in a tent, rose early, worked all day, and loved it. "Oh yeah," he says, "five o'clock in the morning, the sun wouldn't be over the hill then, but you could see the rays. Then it would come over the hill, and it wouldn't be hot, but look just like a big ball of fire. First you'd hear one bird, then you'd hear a couple more, just like an orchestra. We slept in tents—good, fresh air. That was great."

Across the Connecticut River at Mary Hitchcock Hospital in Lebanon, New Hampshire, Katherine Paul was recovering from appendix surgery. She spent nearly six months in the hospital, receiving letters variably addressed "Katherine Paul" and "Catherine Paul," but always at "Hospital Hanover." They came from her friend Kara Newton, who took great pride in decorating each envelope with flowers and nature scenes, creepy crawly forest bugs and intricate landscapes. Katherine treasured them, keeping them for the rest of her life. She was a lovely and kind woman, I'm told, and upon discharge went to work for the Veteran's Affairs Hospital in White River Junction—where she met Joe Pogar.

"It used to be Catherine with a 'C,' but Katherine Hepburn spelled her name with a K, so..." Joe explains, smiling kindly at the memory of his late wife. She was born on February 29th of a leap year, and Joe remembers her as quite the character well befitting her novel birthday.

In those days he lived at the Jameson house, on the corner of the VA's lot there in the quiet part of White River Junction. "There's a filling station over by the VA," he said. "There are two houses there. Now it's built up …but just north of there, a big yellow house." The Jamesons had two daughters, Dorothy and Gladys, whom he recalls fondly.

"Joe knows all the history," Winona chides. "He remembers all the women, and all their names!" Which is true: Joe remembers Kara Newton and the envelopes she made for Katherine, he remembers the Jameson sisters, Dorothy Mock (who I met as Dot Jones) playing basketball and how her uncle Willis married Katherine's sister—the local history and connections one picks up over time. Joe is a charmer, but he's modest.

"Yeah," he said, "I knew the slacks."

He lived at the Jameson house only a short while, between life in the tents and when the crews completed construction on more permanent housing for the staff. The hospital was a mile from downtown White River Junction, where dozens of trains roared through daily. Their traffic was down following the Great Depression, but he still heard steam whistles and distant rumbling as part of the background to everyday White River Junction. The foreground, though, was a bit more interesting.

There was Lena's Lunch on the "rough side of town," a place known to get seedy after dark—where illegal gambling, a holdover from the Prohibition days, was routinely raided by authorities. The Polka Dot and Mayfair restaurants were lively, and the hotels did steady business. "The beds never cool at the Hotel Coolidge," read a beautiful double entendre in one history of the hotel, the source of which I have forgotten—but not the words. Joe courted the lovely Katherine Paul, and played music in taverns and ballrooms around the area. "Ayup," he said, "it was quite a town. It was wild. But the next town was Wilder!"

And so he slips one past those who aren't on their game, as admittedly I wasn't, sitting there scratching notes for the future when I should have been savoring the present. Joe's sense for humor is akin to a wrestler feeling his way carefully, moving so deftly, so coyly, you are unaware of being set up until the punch line pins you square in the moment. Across the White River and up a hill from the wild town of White River Junction is, in fact, the village of Wilder. To add irony to the mix, it has never been much more than a sleepy mill town high above the bustle.

Winona offers us tea, and I readily accept. "It's Tetley's British Blend," she says by way of caution, "so it's going to be very strong." I like strong tea. I enjoy bold tastes and complicated flavors, in a way somewhat akin to how I enjoy strong personalities and complicated people. Joe's character is not as forceful as many; rather, it is complicated in subtle ways. I enjoy hearing his stories and seeing his quirks. It would be over-simplifying and trite to liken the man to tea, or wine, but at the same time, there are commonalities I appreciate—certain subtleties about his vintage.

The living room being more to Joe's liking for afternoon tea, I follow slowly behind as he leads me by memory from the kitchen back into the room where he played his fiddle for me. A slightly dusty, blue easy chair awaits him. I find a rocking chair by the window overlooking his driveway, and settle down eye-level with the wooden ledge that runs around the room separating the wood paneling down low from the white plaster higher up. Along the ledge are snow globes, a small toy race car, tiny teacups, salt and pepper shakers, and the like—the things one accumulates and doesn't quite know what to do with. Winona brings in a jar of cookies and I eat while Joe picks up where he thinks he left off.

"And then, February '41, Uncle Sam says 'I need you, boy,'" he explains. The government drafted him into the US Army as one of the first two-thousand World War II draftees; he was thirty-two, too old for combat training but suited for a support role as the war effort geared up.

"I guess they probably figured they'd have to have cooks and people working the hospital because of casualties," so he was assigned in his familiar role: cook. Based out of Boston, he worked for the VA hospital as a member of the United States Army until they assigned him other temporary duties. One included cooking in the mess car for a train that took wounded soldiers from Boston to their hometowns across the northern and northwestern states.

"The farthest I got was Spokane, Washington," he says very matter-of-factly. "I cooked on the train that was transporting wounded veterans from the east coast to the west coast. I went by way of Minnesota, straight north. Went to Montana, Idaho, Wyoming," he adds, smiling after he said it as if he had a minor revelation right there. "But, Dave, I've had a good life." Of all the things he is wont to repeat, that, perhaps, is his mantra.
250

The Pogar family includes other veterans, as his two uncles served in World War I—a conflict he remembers from childhood. "I was about ten years old," he says, then his eyes darken and he falls quiet as if that sparked other memories he would rather not recall. I don't press.

Though he never fought, unlike his uncles and so many men of the World War generations he knew, he displays the tools of the trade with a certain patriotic flair. Behind his chair, over a potbelly stove that is not connected to a flue (it serves as convincing decoration alone), hang two crossed bayonets from the early part of the twentieth century. "My brother in law, he gave me some of those, in WWII." He used to display them outside, in the lawn near his flagpole, around Independence Day—but the centerpiece of that display was quite a bit larger.

"You know, fourth of July, I have a cannon. It has an inch and a half bore, barrel's about this long. I used to put it out there. I have a German helmet, and an American helmet, and I'd take these swords (bayonets) and I'd poke 'em alongside. And somewheres along I had a bullet about six inches long. And American flags and so on. A little lad down the street, he'd come up, and wanted to know all about it. Back in those days, nobody would steal it. I could put it on the lawn and leave it there overnight. But not now," he says with disappointment.

Back in those days, he could fire it in a field right across the street. "So one day I loaded it up," and his cheer is suddenly back, "and put a fuse in. I lighted it. And my wife's cousin lived up the road a bit, and he heard it! So he come running down with some slugs, and said 'put these in it!' So I put in three slugs and

251

charged it up. I had it pointed over across the water. I didn't have it elevated enough to carry over, but I could see where it ended up across the river. And that thing jumped about a foot in the air!" Perhaps Wilder was a little bit wild after all.

President Eisenhower's interstate highway system came through Vermont in the 1950s, connecting the quaint villages with the surrounding country by car, without the limitations of train travel. A celebration in Montpelier marked the joining of the interstate segments into a contiguous road through Vermont that connected Massachusetts with Burlington; Joe's cannon attended the ceremony. "The agents from the BATFE (then called the Bureau of Alcohol, Tobacco, Firearms and Explosives, now shortened to "ATF") came up and they wanted to know why I had the cannon. It was during the Cold War with Russia, and they inquired about it." But nothing came of the matter. Joe was just a patriotic World War II veteran, after all—a man who served his country, and wasn't likely to take his relic and attack his own homeland.

The situation was farcical: the cannon, the ceremony, the BATFE interrogating a war veteran in the corner...Joe regards it with appropriate levity. His laugh right now is the kind I have after getting away with something— whether it was actually against the rules or not. When you listen to the Green Mountains, you can hear that sort of laugh mix with steam whistles and bucksaws in the wind.

Joe was based out of the VA Hospital, where he worked as part of the Army until 1945 and then as a civilian for the rest of his career. He saw Katherine between train trips, and 1942 found him living happily in White River Junction…and getting ready for a rather important day that summer: Joe and Katherine were married July 9th. They moved into 46 Passumpsic Avenue, which was owned by Katherine's family, and started their family almost exactly nine months later with the April 7th birth of Joseph Junior. Marcia was born in July of 1944, and in 1945 Joe purchased the home from his brother-in-law.

Joe's longstanding service to the VA Hospital put him in better financial standing as a new father than his immigrant father had managed in the '20s. With only one brother, John, Joe's family remained small by early 1900s Vermont standards…yet it was the largest they could afford to care for.

In better circumstances with their household, Joe and Katherine made a larger family—a Vermont-sized, close knit family. In 1945, Katherine's father William died, and her mother Mary moved in with the young couple. They had three more children, William in '49, Mary in '51, and Debbie in '53, to total five children, two parents, and grandma living together in the Passumpsic Avenue home. The eight filled the two-story home, and made do thanks to their creativity and their parents' experience with Great Depression thrift. Katherine tended a garden out back, Mary canned the family's produce, and Joe managed the finances.

"We had a family budget," he explains. By then Joe, who Winona reminds me is a high school dropout, had risen at the VA to become Chief of Finance. "I wish I had kept (a copy of that budget), I threw it away. You know, I think we bought 150 quarts of milk in one month!" He laughs, and I imagine him sitting alone in his kitchen now with a hundred-fifty quarts of milk.

They ate well, he said—a sure measure of wealth and security in rural Vermont those days—and the children were well looked after by Katherine and Mary. The women canned corn and tomatoes, a supply of which filled the basement for decades—Winona helped Joe throw the last of them out in 2004. The women left their legacy in the Pogar home, from the muted echoes of children's laughter to the basement full of preserves, to the handmade commemorative plate hanging on the wall in the living room.

Mary Paul, Katherine's mother, was moderately skilled with pottery and took pride in making a commemorative plate for each of her children upon their weddings. Joe and Katherine's plate hangs carefully on the wall near a cabinet in the corner. The Polish Eagle commands the center while their names and wedding date are written carefully around the edge. "She used to make vases, jars, things of that sort," he said. "In fact, I've got a kiln, a potter's wheel and a kiln, in the basement," that were hers.

The plate hangs near a sepia tone photograph of Katherine that shows a beautiful woman with dark hair and a mischievous smile—a smile that suggests she never lost her inner child. The photograph is tucked behind a small porcelain tea set in a display cabinet brimming with jars and cups, a glass rose in a crystal ball, and bric-a-brac by the bushel. Everything has a story, though some are quite simple.

"There was a fad, (collecting) jugs and bottles," Joe says to explain the jugs, bottles, cups and similar things sprinkled along the rail and throughout the open spaces in the room. "I should have gone through this stuff back when I was able to see..." He probably would have kept most of it anyway—he has kept his daughters' dolls and a few stuffed toys since the 1950s, his late wife's bottles and jugs, the sentimental bric-a-brac with the attachments that grow stronger with time... no, he would not likely have thrown much away had he tried. From the nostalgia in his voice, to the old toys, to Katherine's letters from Kara Newton that he keeps in a plastic Ziploc bag, Joe proves to be a rather sentimental guy.

I look around the room and inventory Joe Pogar's life—there is the piano to my left, with stacks of sheet music on the music stand, and recessed shelves in the wall behind it. There is a Howdy Doody doll on one shelf, and a glass insulator like they used on power lines many years ago. To the right are a doorway and a tall, wide, shallow display case filled with single-serving alcohol bottles. One is in the shape of a violin, and reading the label, contains Vermont maple syrup.

I glance over the rows and rows of tiny Drambuie and Jameson bottles, and only then notice that he has grown quiet. "That's quite the collection of mini-bottles there," I say to abate the silence.

"These bottles are replicas of the big bottles, you know," he says with unexpected interest. "But they're drying out, evaporating. I used to go on airplanes. Then they used to give you a little nip. They don't do it now, I guess." Winona brings our tea and sits just out of the way between us.

"That's for his wake!" she says, laughing. "He says, when we have the wake, we'll pass those out!"

"Stand me up in the corner, they could dance with me!" he says with whimsy.

"Take me around the room," I say, "and tell me

about the things here that you've made." But instead of the things, he starts telling me about the place.

"You know, back until 1950," he explains, "there weren't too many houses here. New England Power, they built five homes for their employees." The nearby International Paper Mill had built the existing homes earlier in the century; his was one of those. "(This is) one of the better built ones. This house has brick inside, between the outside and the inside wall there's brick all the way up. It had old-fashioned wiring. I rewired the house, and had a tough time with that." He mentions things like *when I rewired the house* so smoothly, so unprepossessingly that you almost miss it—the high school dropout, head of finance for the hospital, accomplished musician, also rewired this house. I know people who are hard-pressed to change light bulbs, and he rewired the building...and now, he seems not to think much of it. This understated way of presenting himself without brash boasting is familiar from Harold, Larry, and Dot. "To get a box in," he continues, "I had to chisel out the brick there. It's a good old, sturdy house."

The house first held the William Goss family, whose son left his marks—they can still be seen in the wooden doors in the living room wall behind Joe. "The son, he was a wild guy, he had a tantrum and broke every window in the house," and punched out many of the recessed wood panels in the interior doors. There are still cracks from his fists, cracks that remember him though he is now long dead. Joe's children are still alive, scattered around the country (Joe Jr. is a decorated fireman in California), and remembered by the toys on the trim and the small artifacts—photos and trinkets Joe can no longer see—strewn about the home. And, of course, by the kitchen that Joe Jr. and his father built onto the house. Joe is aware that someday the objects and the additions will be all that is left to mark their claim in the house's history. "There'll come a day, Dave," he acknowledges, "when there'll be other little feet running here. But it's been a good home."

He tries to change the subject, as he is prone to change topics out of humility and honestly not knowing what more I want to learn. Lest we prematurely leave the subject of marking, of claiming, space I goad him into telling me a bit more. His children left their marks too, he says, as the house became their home. How?

Most notably, Joe Jr. helped build the kitchen that extends now from the living room towards the trees lining the far edge of the backyard. "Originally, where that beam was," he says, pointing overhead, "this was the kitchen. In here." The booze cabinet was made of an old cupboard, a couch was in front of what is now the entrance to the kitchen, and there was another cabinet behind where the piano sits.

"This was in the summer time," he continues. "I had Joe help me put that addition on. Joe came home from work and was all excited about something, and said 'come on, let's go!' So we went up there and worked until about ten. Then he said 'I'm tired,' so I said 'we ought to put a tarp over the roof, it's open, it's just rafters.' Well, if it rains, that plywood would separate. 'Oh, it's not going to rain.' Well, about three o'clock I woke up alarmed and wet! I woke him up and said 'Hey, Jesus man, it's raining!' So we put the tarp up, and the water filled the tarp between the rafters. So I made a cross-T, and when that thing would fill, I'd push it up and drain it. The rest of the night I stayed up and

257

dumped the water out. Then I took all that Sunday to rest."

There were plenty of carpenters who could have built onto the house, but money was tight with most of his five children still at home—and Joe could do it. The self-taught Chief of Finance, the self-taught professional cook, the self-taught musician and self-made man knew enough about carpentry to make it work.

The addition looks seamless. With a new kitchen, the old kitchen became a comfortable living room and performance space when Joe dragged the upright piano in from the family room just down the hall. Together, the Pogar men had added their flourish to the Goss home. Over the years, the new living room and kitchen slowly filled with things that reflected Joe and Katherine—many of which he built.

So I ask him about the wooden table near his chair, one with simple spindle legs—each leg has three perfectly aligned, carved bands. He runs his hand over the brown top, pats it once, and thanks me for complimenting the craftsmanship.

"That's when you have good eyesight," he says like he's joking—but he's not, really. He turned those legs on his lathe, back when his hands could make anything his eyes could measure. He kept working after he could no longer see the beauty of his craft, and his hands still know their ways around wood and tools.

"I've got too many chairs, too many things," he laments halfheartedly; indeed the room is filled with the sort of keepsakes and furniture and *that's too good to throw out* –type things people accumulate. Some are useful, others are not, and some lost their utility but linger—like the pipe-stand beside his chair. There are no pipes in it, and he doesn't smoke anymore.

"I had a cold here a little while ago, and I decided to give it up," he says of pipe smoking. He gave it up at ninety-seven—after fifty years of smoking that began at the behest of a coworker.

"When I was about forty-two, working at the VA, the auditor came up. I had plenty of time on my hands, I always did my work and then I'd have spare time. He said 'you ought to have a pipe,' so I went down to the canteen and got a pipe. 'I'll show you how to break it in.' I was forty-two years old at the time, and I smoked until, well, in the service I smoked a lot of times, but I enjoyed it. Sitting around with a pipe, it's like a pacifier for adults."

In 1950, most everyone smoked—Winona smoked, as did her husband, the other workers at the VA Hospital, and even Katherine. She died in the 1980s, from cancer. After more than four decades of marriage, Joe was a widower—and still smoked, packing the occasional bowl with tobacco from a can inside that pipe stand.

There are so many stories attached to the things we own—the things we make, the things we buy, the stuff with which we surround ourselves. Hearing the stories behind the possessions is fascinating—what does it mean, or could it mean, or should it mean? I hear stories that seem familiar to my life, of looking for a wife, of working jobs I never expected to have, of leaving my hometown to build a life elsewhere...many of the stories are universal, which is comforting.

There is something to be said for laughing at a foible we know too well from common mistakes in separate lives, and in seeing how someone else faced a challenge we unknowingly shared. Talking with Joe seems less like interviewing someone about the formula that produced their personality—the combination of successes and failures, and the influence of their era and surroundings—and more like reuniting with a lost friend.

Joe didn't make that pipe stand, but many other things in his home came out of his basement workshop. They bear the tiny scratches and imperfections that prove they were made by hand, the sort of things that mark each as uniquely his, like fingerprints. But not everything he built is here in the home—a dry sink he made followed his grandchildren through the expanding Pogar family, and his lamps light several homes. Through his crafts, he is present in each of his children's lives—small pieces of the man who loves them all.

"I remember one time, when Mary's little girl was small, I built a table and two chairs," he recalls. Winona offers a postscript.

"Marcia said that Jesse took the table and is using it as a coffee table at his apartment in Boston," she explains. The furniture Joe makes stays in the family, passed between siblings or stored for safekeeping in an era when furniture is bought and sold almost every time someone moves—but the things he makes are special, from their uncommon strength and quality to how each is imbued with care and a sense of pride. In an increasingly disposable world where furniture is made to be cheap and light, disposable after only an owner or two, the feel of solid oak and hand-sanded pine, real varnish and linseed oil—and a father's touch—is something truly special.

"We're living too fast," he says. There is nothing fast about making your own furniture, and with the time and effort invested, folks are likely to take much better care of it than the soulless products of mass production—"heirloom quality" is a special feature now, or a phrase we use to describe the things our great grandparents made.

They didn't use those words; they just called it "good," and used the thing for the rest of their lives. "I don't know what it's going to be like twenty years from now," he continues. "We need a depression," or something to remind us of the worth of hard work and the value of a dollar. "This country needs a straightening up, it's going to hell." Here he slips into a stereotype—of a tired old man complaining about change—but somehow manages to shirk it off almost as quickly as I place it upon him; Joe is not a grizzled old curmudgeon, though his words are harsh on this subject.

Rather, his words are harsh because he cares about his grandchildren and their futures, so he denounces the direction of social norms and changing values he sees as threats to their wellbeing. Looking back on a successful, happy life, it must be hard to imagine any other set of circumstances that could produce his same security and contentedness; thus, any new paradigm must seem frightening. Perhaps this is the case with Joe's fear for my future; perhaps though he, having seen so much, now sees legitimate problems I can't.

"You know, Dave, I may sound awful to say this," he continues, "but I've been preaching and praying a depression for a year or two, to get this country back." During the last depression people traded potatoes for clothes and other food—trading things they worked to grow for things they needed to live. "They had gardens. They would exchange, instead of dollars, potatoes.

261

(Something like that now) would save the land, and also put people to work."

Now there's a concept that defines the Great Depression generation, that defines Vermonters, and surely defines Joe Pogar: work. Attention to detail—from his job as Chief of Finance to playing note-perfect music. Making something of oneself—like a Polish immigrant starting with the coins in his pocket and building a life and family in a brave new world. These are values he holds, values he sees are critical to the country—and values he believes have fallen by the wayside.

I believe him, though I held similar ideas and made related observations before meeting Joe; perhaps I'm just a twenty-something curmudgeon. Perhaps we're both onto something.

"But Dave," he finishes, "all I can say is, the life ahead of you, you can do a lot of things. Keep busy. Of course you have to be adapted to something, be it arts or crafts or writing, whatever, but you have to have some goal in life."

Joe's jobs, and even his hobbies, have always involved goals, focus, and hard work: the physical labor kind like carpentry, or the kind that take dedication and practice like music. More than just dedicated action, though, they tend to require a balance between precision and craftsmanship—like following recipes while knowing how they can be changed as needed.

Good musicians can follow sheet music perfectly, but great musicians know when, and how, to improvise. In his construction, Joe shows flair for technical accuracy (angles that should be ninety degrees, are) while making room for the flourishes of a master craftsman—the bands on the legs, the stencils, the scaled-down table and chairs for Mary's daughter... Joe is a true craftsman, with bright creativity and the lingering strength from a life lived working. I make a comment to that effect.

"Yeah, well..." he says, smiling. "I'll show you some of the things that I miss doing," and he reaches for a small box by his chair. He pulls from it a square of wood with dark-stained plastic on one side, carved away to make a nativity scene. "See this here, Dave?" he says with a twinkle in his eye, and I recognize the pattern as the reverse of a Christmas card the town Lister showed me several months ago.

"Oh yeah!" I say. "I've seen a print made by that, actually!" I'm proud of recognizing it, surprised and happy to make the immediate connection to Joe...who looks suddenly crestfallen.

"You have?" He says, voice fading. "Where'd you see that?"

"In the Lister's office," and then I made my second mistake. "With your poem inside!" It was a very nice poem, too, and well written.

"Oh." I immediately regret saying anything. "You stole my thunder," he tries to joke, but the energy has passed. The plastic, he explains at my urging, like a bored teacher covering a basic topic yet again, is cut away to leave the raised image.

"Well, you get a blank piece of linoleum block," he goes on. "The print I got from the newspaper. You know, around Christmas time they have a lot of religious pictures and so on. In here somewheres I've got my carving tools," he says, rooting through the box, showing me tiny chisels and a small knife. "Just carve a groove in there, ya know, and then just... there's no

263

limit to what you can learn." He would ink the stamp and press it upon blue construction paper, write his poem inside, and mail the card to friends and family—cheaper than buying cards, more special, and it gave him a great project on which to work.

His also painted, using a calendar for inspiration to make several roughly identical paintings. From my seat I can see, upon the front wall above an overflowing collection of cassette tapes—country western music, Bing Crosby, and the like—the black and white silhouette painting of a cowboy set within a barn wood frame. "I painted the silhouette there," he explains, rising from his chair. "I did about six of them. A carpenter gave me a calendar, and I just had to enlarge it. It's not quite perfect, the man is a little too big. If it was perfect, then it wouldn't be worth as much," he jokes with the twinkle back in his blind eyes; he looks so energetic now—so young.

His eldest daughter has one of those cowboy paintings of his, on canvas—"the real one," he explains. We're on our feet now, walking past the booze cabinet and through a short hallway.

"Dave, I've changed this place," he leads, and I follow by asking oh? "This is a bathroom that I built, and a little corner cupboard I made."

Winona is behind me now, wearing the grey sweater and smiling, chiming in "We made!" She had helped him with the shelf when he needed sharper eyes; it was one of her earliest projects with him, of which there have been many.

On our left is a small laundry room with a bathroom on one side and a shelf built into the corner. Without his mention, I would not have guessed that this room

264

had been added to the original structure—the floor is seamless at the threshold, the proportions look just right and there is little to suggest that the open doorway had once been an exterior wall. A window overlooks the backyard. "And that's my little doggie out there," he says, pointing instinctively straight out the window. Hartford Sunny was her show name, Winona explains—a little Pekinese he came to call Honey. "I lost her a year and a half ago. She was the nicest little thing. I buried her out back."

We move on.

"I tell ya, I've got a mess here," he says, walking me into a family room at the end of the hall. "But what I don't see doesn't bother me!" There is a twin-size bed along the wall, musical instrument cases, boxes, file folders and the like strewn everywhere; but it's an ordered chaos, the sort that makes sense...to Joe at least. Music lies upon instrument cases, envelopes atop folders, arranged in the room like I can easily conceive they are arranged in his mind...and who can differentiate order from mess in another man's mind?

"I've got music, but I've got to get going some day," he says. "Here's a cello, a banjo, I've got a mandolin, six fiddles. You ever seen an electric fiddle?" I should not have said yes. "Oh," he says. Again I have pulled the wind from his sails, and a moment too late is a moment too late indeed as I long desperately to call back my words. He would have enjoyed showing off his electric fiddle, perhaps playing a few chords, telling a few stories...what had I just lost?

"You know, anything electronic is not like the original," he explains. "Especially, when I play with a hearing aid, it's harsh; it's not like the real sound. I have to adjust that," and his words come heavy with lassitude. "But anyway…" He feels around on a crowded table and picks up a small digital clock, presses a button, and a canned voice says *eleven thirty eight*—he's adaptable.

"And here Dave, everything I told you about. Here's a thing I made," he says, setting the clock down upon a wooden dresser. He pulls out the top drawer and I am impressed by the perfect notching of the wood, the interlocking teeth that hold the drawer together without screws. On the front of the drawer is a simple, black design with red bells stenciled upon the wood. "I made one, and the kids said 'hey dad, make me one!' So I did."

"Hey," there's that energy back in his voice, "did I ever show you my electric fiddle?" *No…would you?* That was definitely the right answer. "Ok!" He shuffles sideways to the far end of the bed, where he finds a black padded case and tells me how to open the right compartment. Inside is a fine, stylized fiddle made of laminated wood with knobs, four strings and a plug in the bottom for the audio cable. I can't imagine a ninety-eight year old man rocking out on such an instrument, but he grabs it and pulls it out of the case with positively youthful pride. This isn't the reverence he showed patting the furniture he made, or in holding his traditional fiddle. No, this newfangled thing brought him straight into the modern era and he knows it. He offers it to me, and I put it to my collarbone, settling my chin upon the chin rest and sighting the pegbox right down the fingerboard—it is obvious I have no idea what I am doing. But it feels good.

We put it away, with no stories or revelations, just the smile on the old man's face to belie that something is going on in his mind—some evaluation, or memory, or dream, or whatever it is that makes him smile earnestly as he slips the case beneath the bed and shuffles towards the front door. A stairway leads up to the second floor, where Mary Paul lived with her daughter and son-in-law after her husband died. Tracing the ceiling all the way up is a simple black trim of bells with red appointments— more of his handiwork. "I plastered this wall," he says, fishing around in a waxed paper bag hanging from the handle of the front door. "They don't do it today, they use wallboard. This is real plaster. Then I did the trim, all the way up. That stenciling goes all the way up and around there." He hands me an apple that has obviously been in the bag awhile, but is still plenty good. "It's good for you. It's a little shriveled up. Take it, an apple a day keeps the doctor away." His asides amuse me.

"Plastering, that's a tough job." Back on track, we walk into the living room and find our seats amidst the cups of cooling tea and coffee.

"You have to do it in a couple courses," he continues. "You put down a ground course, then you level it, then you put on a white finish course." And I wonder, for a moment, why he didn't just hire a plasterer to come and…but that's not how Joe thinks. His perspectives come from times—the Great Depression and World War II with its rationing—when there was neither money to hire someone, nor any perceived need—there is no limit to what a man can learn, as he points out. When Joe needed an addition to the house, he built it; when he needed a table or a cabinet, he built it. His only obstacle was not knowing how to do a thing, and that was easily rectified by trying and learning.

He doesn't think this is special—it's just the way

things are to him and a generation of self-reliant men and women who could can tomatoes as well as they could change a tire or raise a child. "What do they say," he adds, "necessity is the mother of invention? Well, if I needed something, I'd make it." He finds it shameful that today so many people hire out work for even the simplest things. I agree, while recognizing that the scope of our ambitions is somewhat different—I have plastered walls and built furniture, but probably won't rewire my house. Winona used to be one of those people who hire out basic tasks; before she met Joe, anyway.

"There was a problem with the vent for the heater downstairs," she explains. "I told him, 'Joe, we need to get a guy here to fix it,' but he said 'no we can do it ourselves.'" All they needed was a single sheet metal screw to hold the vent together, and Joe to direct her where to fasten it. The repair holds to this day.

"Winona, she's pretty good now, you know," he surmises. She plays piano, fixes circuit breakers, works with tools...most all of which she learned under his tutelage. "I have to go down to Staples and get a blank certificate form, and give her a certificate of workmanship," he says chivalrously. "She's a, she's pretty handy. She's my helper."

"I couldn't do it when my husband was alive," she says. "He would always do it. Then he died, and I had to learn." And so they make a dynamic team, Winona describing problems—electrical, mechanical—to Joe, who diagnoses them and guides her through the solution. He taught her how to use power tools, and together they built one of the cabinets in the kitchen, the corner shelf in the laundry room, and more. He helped her discover new independence, new freedom by being more self-reliant. A Vermonter born and raised, Winona proved an apt pupil—she wanted to learn as much as Joe wanted to teach.

"But I'd never done anything like that," she says, "so Joe would say 'do this, and measure that,' and then Joe would make the saw go, and oh boy! He would tell me how long to measure, and how to cut it…" Her face glows with that inspiring sense of power people get when they learn something difficult—when they gain confidence from experience, and believe in themselves. There is, indeed, no limit to what you can learn—or when you can learn it.

"They warned me, my kids, 'keep away from those things,'" Joe says, sadness in his voice. Winona keeps talking, cheerfully.

"He'd say 'drill it here,' and 'nail it there,' and it's pretty good for someone who can't see to tell someone who doesn't know anything about it how to get things done. But he did these things when he could see."

"Yeah, we made some stuff, huh?" he finishes, with a big brother's smile—and that haunting twinge of melancholy. She was his eyes and he was her teacher as she caught up on a lifetime of practical knowledge… and discovered new faith in herself.

But they can no longer build the cabinets and tables and other projects; the tools are gone. Winona explains, "We were going to work some more, but the kids said 'oh no,' and took the equipment, so Joe only has one saw down there."

You can understand their concern over their ninety-eight year old father, living alone and effectively blind, still using power tools; but despite the good intentions, it still feels mean. "And the saw, it doesn't work," she finishes, explaining "somebody cut the cord on it last summer." And so another era passed for a man who has seen so many pass already.

"Joe always says, 'oh, you can do this,' 'oh, you can do that!'" she beams, with as much pride in herself as gratitude for her mentor. That is how she discovered playing music, she says—how she came from having no background in music to accompanying Joe on the piano.

"She'd never had any musical training," Joe explains, "but I've got a piano, so she came here and heard me play. She got this book, and I kind of reversed it. It's called 'Piano for Dummies,' but I think it's 'Dummies for Piano.'" It was funnier in person—really.

"She plays chords, and that's all I want," he says. And she plays well, he adds; I agree, based on the songs I heard. Perhaps her patience—with herself, and with him—is her biggest resource. It takes awhile to learn how to read music, and without the help of an instructor who can see, she was largely on her own beyond his pointers.

"I can't read music anymore," he explains, using the obvious to set a stage for an anecdote. "There's a woman from Hanover I used to play with, but she would say 'you're not playing it right!' That's okay, I play it according to the measures and the chords and so on." His bitterness is veiled rather well, but I can tell that she hurt him. As his eyes failed, he held firmly to what he knew, what could never be taken away by a lack of sight—his music, played by memory and feel. It was a big comfort, something he could do despite his age and eyes failing, and to be told that he wasn't "playing it right," must have cut him to the bone. He quit

270

playing with her, resigning himself to evermore private rehearsals…but then he met Winona and took her under his wing, helping her discover new talents and vocations as she helped him keep up with daily challenges.

And gave him another reason to keep playing the music he loves so much.

She changes his hearing aid batteries, and makes him tea. More often than not, he pays for lunch when they go to the Bugbee Senior Center, China Moon, or the other restaurants just down the hill in White River Junction. I mention the Tip Top Café in the old Smith & Sons Bakery building, and he seems interested. "Yeah," he says, "it's about time for lunch, isn't it? 'Nona, what are you in the mood for?"

"The senior center has, oh, let me think," she says, adjusting the grey sweater, "it has ravioli today. But that place, that sounds good, do you want to go, Joe?"

"Yeah, where's that at, Dave?"

"North Main Street, the…"

"Ward Baking Company? They've got a restaurant in there now? Jeez." They do indeed. "Yeah, we could go."

"Now is there anything else you want to tell him?" she asks, for which I'm grateful. "He wanted to know about connections to the town," Winona continues. "You want to tell him about the dam, the old bridge you went across?"

I'm more interested in the Tip Top Building—part of why I suggested we go there for lunch, to see if wandering through the building triggers any interesting memories—but this tangent about the dam could be interesting too. Tangents are distractions by their very definition, but I'm convinced that we don't follow nearly enough of them—who knows what you might learn down a sidetrack.

Besides, there seem to be fewer and fewer front porches and Indian summers, fewer long winter mornings in cozy Vermont homes, fewer times when we can follow a good tangent for all it's worth. The tangent's direction itself shows as much about the person—where they take it, and why—as what they actually say. They give two lessons in one, and are hardly the frivolity they seem at first. I have learned so much so far this morning, asking questions and unobtrusively listening—just listening, to whatever Joe has to say. So I nod my head and smile, and Joe takes me back in time again.

"I had a picture of the old rail station down there," he says. "According to history, I don't know if it's true or not, but Roger's Rangers came up through. And I guess he lost a boat or something. Said when they dredged part of the Connecticut, they found a bunch of rifles, pretty well preserved." Sometimes tangents don't illuminate the dark mysteries of the soul; sometimes they're just interesting.

"I've got a book," Joe continues. "One chapter tells about a guy from Forks, Maine. He was a construction worker. His father was a guide, a hunter, and so on. But he worked for contractors, and he worked on this dam down here," the Wilder Dam, used by New England Power to create hydroelectricity just a few dozen yards from Joe's living room. "And he said when they diverted the river, they found logs down there that had been down there for I don't know how long. But they were in the water, so they didn't rot, so someone took 'em to the mill and they were just as good as the day they were cut."

272

Unfortunately, he was still a boy in New York when the last of the mighty log drives flowed down the untamed Connecticut in the 1920s—I can only imagine how he would have described seeing those logs filling the river on their way towards the sea. They floated past this home, in the river just across the street. It would have been an amazing sight.

Now, views of the river are obscured by the houses on the far side of the street, a row not yet as dense as a suburb, but filling—changing—nonetheless. It makes him somewhat territorial, and after sixty-four years at the same address, he has a spiritual claim to the street. "I've got a nice lot down there," nearer the water, he says. "I hate to think that somebody's going to dig it up and put a house there. When I first came here, there were about twenty homes. Now there's about forty. And it's not necessary."

While the setting is distinctly Vermont, his passion for protecting his land—protecting the way things are—is universal. I have seen it in Harold Wright's resistance to selling his land, and in Dot Jones maintaining the family home that is far larger than she and Lorna need. Vermonters are especially proud of their land and its natural beauty, and especially resistant to either being changed…but again, that's not solely a Vermont thing. I'm not a Vermonter, and can relate; so can a lot of people. Perhaps this common ground could be the starting point for something.

"All the land here is at a premium," he continues. "When I go, they're gonna—you be against it! You tell 'em you don't want it. I'd like to go down there and get permission to have an animal cemetery there, and put my stone right there in the middle. Old Joe…" He's serious…mostly.

Being buried in a certain plot of land is as intimate a connection with a place as one could want—the ultimate claim to stake. "This is home," he says, "and I'm going to stay here." And though he is smiling now, joking a little, there is certainly an underlying truth in his words about the connection he feels with the land. This home is his; this street, the mountains and the river and this Town of Hartford where he has worked and lived for seventy years are his…and he, in turn, is theirs. The New York musician has become a Vermonter.

What is it about change that we embrace when we are young, and resist so vehemently as we grow old? Perhaps it's a valuation of stability, perhaps it's in identifying with the way things have been—the way we have been—that feels intimately threatened by changing circumstances. When the things that we identify with the most change, must we change as well? Should we?

The number 208 still hangs on his garage, the old address before the numbers changed with the introduction of 911 and emergency management. Elsewhere he has the number 46 tacked up, showing the "new" address; in the next room rests his electric fiddle, that modern spin on an old instrument. Joe submits to the changing times, but remains dedicated to his wood stoves and personal philosophies; a cloud of wood smoke in the winter air, warm and rising and defiant and ephemeral. He holds onto the stories and traditions that formed him, and now when he sits in the sunlight before his front windows, he thinks what a shame it is to have this Green Mountain neighborhood—his neighborhood—develop into just another stretch of houses.

And so we finish our tea and wipe the crumbs away,

and Winona trades the grey sweater for her coat. She folds it in her lap, pats it once along the crease, and answers my inquiring eyes. There must be something to that sweater—and there is. "This is an old sweater I found on Joe's cellar floor," she says, smiling; it was Katherine's, which does not bother either she or Joe. "So I wear it whenever I'm over here." It makes her as much a part of the place as the pictures on the wall and the chairs around the room—which is to say that by wearing something from Joe's life, found upon the floor of his home, she physically becomes a part of each. It fits that the two women so important in Joe's life should be linked across time and circumstance by a garment that warms and comforts Winona during her time with Joe. I follow them through the kitchen, don my winter warmest, and step through the door into the Vermont late morning.

I drive ahead of Winona's car, leading them down the hill into White River Junction and then left down North Main Street to the Tip Top Building. We park, and I describe the renovations and current architecture to Joe. I point out the arched brick window frames and recessed, encircled crosses in the stones high above on many of George Smith's buildings downtown. Joe remembers those details, but has never connected them before—never noticed how those details reflect one man's lasting influence on many buildings and an entire downtown.

The Tip Top Café is just now opening, so I give Joe and Winona a quick tour of the building while we have time. I read the signs to Joe, *As illustration of the extent of Mr. Smith's cracker making*, so he feels included in the sightseeing.

We walk over the threshold between wooden floor and concrete, and I explain the story of the buildings being joined over time into one huge structure. I tell him of the building's rise and fall, and he nods and says "uh huh," and "I remember when they used to have Tip Top Tire in here," and "didn't there used to be a guy by the name of…"

We walk on, Winona reading the signs hanging outside artists' studios and pasted near pieces of art in the hallway while I narrate what I remember of the building's history. "I've never been in here before," he says, clasping his hands upon the top of his cane. "It's good, you know, see an old building get used." We trade smiles, because we know that buildings are a lot like people—if they don't get proper use, they crumble into the earth.

It happened along Railroad Row, and it happens in nursing homes across the country. But this building and this man are different—Joe has Winona, and the friends he plays violin for at the Bugbee Senior Center. His children live all over the country, but they keep in touch. He endures his failed eyesight and hearing, and takes them in stride as well as one can hope. Winona is a part of that—his chauffeur, his accompanist, his friend.

"C'mon Dave, let's get some food," he says, having his fill of living in the past. Lunchtime is upon White River Junction; there will be other mornings to learn about history. Now it is time to share the present with a new friend. Joe holds open the door to the Tip Top Café, from which come the strains of piano and violin—the older the fiddle, the sweeter the music, I recall. I catch his eye on my way in, and for a moment there in the music and the doorway I swear he can see me smiling.

Winona, Joe, and the author

Also by Dave Norman

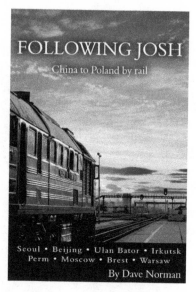

Available Now!

Following Josh is the amazing true story of two men going in opposite directions through life while travelling together from China to Europe by rail. It is a memoir of changing from a twenty-something kid into a married adult, and an amusing tour of the countries, cultures, and history they encountered along the way.

How did Ghengis Khan conquer so much of the world... on horseback? And what's that have to do with Beijing's city planning? Why is paintball the perfect game in Russia, and isn't vodka more Polish than Russian? Following Josh does a tremendous job of illustrating history with anecdote, and weaving deft cultural observations with humor, background, and insight. More than a memoir, more than a history, more than a travelogue, **Following Josh** is a modern adventure story wrapped in a thousand years of history.

www.followingjosh.com

Also by Dave Norman

Leading
Jake

Coming in 2012
from
f/64 Publishing

The adventure continues in **Leading Jake**, where Dave meets his best friend in Krakow — a medieval city with an ancient soul and a youthful lust for life. Their coming-of-age story is set against rich historic and cultural backdrops as they explore Krakow and Prague. Then alone at last in Germany, land of his ancestors, Dave must make peace with former loves and other trauma before embracing a new life.

From absinthe bars to Auschwitz, a fire-breathing dragon's lair to Oktoberfest — and that space between extended adolescence and adulthood — **Leading Jake** is the provocative, laugh-out-loud sequel to **Following Josh** that will inspire you to fall in love with life...and laugh with every breath.

www.f64publishing.com

Acknowledgements

I would like to acknowledge the many people who talked about their town, shared their perspectives and life stories, and helped me make the connections to continue my research. I am grateful for your time, and would like to specially recognize railroad men Mike Farnsworth and Howard Logan, railroad historians Bill Brigham and Chris McKinley, artistic entrepreneur Matt Bucy, and the incomparable David Fairbanks Ford.

Special thanks are in order to Harold and Maxine Wright, Larry Chase, Dot Jones and Lorna Ricard, and Joe Pogar and Winona Hary, for welcoming me into their homes and making history truly come alive.

The essays comprising "White River Junctions" began as distinct projects during my Masters of Arts in Liberal Studies coursework at Dartmouth College. They were edited into the book you're holding, a different project from where the essays began, with unique content and focus...but it all started under the generous direction of Dr. Barbara Kreiger, and was informed by the minds of Alan Lelchuk and Brock Brower, also professors at Dartmouth College at the time. Many thanks to them for helping me shape the original work that ultimately became this book.

Sources

Interviews:

Brigham, Bill. Interview on 9.10.05.
Bucy, Matt. Interview in October 2004.
Farnsworth, Mike. Interview on 9.10.05.
Ford, David F. Interview in October 2004.
Logan, Howard. Interview on 9.10.05.
McKinley, Chris. Interview on 9.22.05.

Websites:

http://ingrimayne.saintjoe.edu/econ/EconomicCatastrophe/GreatDepression.html. Accessed 9.26.05.

www.allbiographies.com/biography-AmmiBurnhamYoung-57526.html. Access on 9.26.05.

www.bergen.org/AAST/Projects/depression/successes.html Accessed on 9.26.05.

www.crjc.org/heritage/V11-8.htm

www.hartfordsd.com/wrs/hartfordti.htm

www.linecamp.com/museums/americanwest/western_clubs/transcontinental_railroad/transcontinental_railroad.html

www.si.edu/opa/insideresearch/9789/89rfd.htm

www.treas.gov/offices/management/curator/exhibitions/
restoration/young_bio.html. Accessed on 9.26.05.

www.wrpaper.com/history.htm

Books and Other Publications:

Bradford, Gamaliel. Biography and the Human Heart.
Cambridge: Houghton Mifflin. 1906.

Doyle, Senator William. "Vermont's Second Statehouse:
200 Years of State Capitol History: Part Two," Vermont
Guardian, August 5th, 2005.

Eastman, Max. Heroes I Have Known. New York, Simon
and Schuster, 1942.

Eddy, Robert. "Bill Brigham Retires From RR," The Herald
of Randolph VT, October 3, 2002.

Ferrarotti, Franco. "On the Autonomy of the Biographical
Method." Biography and Society. Beverly Hills: Sage
Publications. 1981. 19-28.

Gagnon, Nicole. "On the Analysis of Life Accounts."
Biography and Society. Ed. Daniel Bertaux. California:
Sage Publications. 1981. 47-60.

Hallock, R.P. Junior. "Vermont Railroads 1831-1851."
Paper for Professor Hill, Dartmouth College, April 18,
1938.

"Hotel History and Lore," brochure from the Hotel
Coolidge, White River Junction, Vermont. Acquired on
9.23.05.

Jones, Robert C. "The Central Vermont Railway, A Yankee Tradition." Silverton, Colorado: Sundance Publications. Volumes I-V.

Passenger rates: "Woodstock Railroad. Passenger Rates in Effect May 1, 1885."

Sheldon, George. A History of Deerfield, Massachusetts. Greenfield, Massachusetts: E.A. Hall & Co. 1895.

St. Croix, John. Historical Highlights of the Town of Hartford Vermont. Hartford: Imperial Company. 1974.

Tucker, Howard. History of Hartford. Free Press Association. 1889.

Whitehill, Walter. Analecta Biographica; a Handful of New England Portraits. Brattleboro, VT, Stephen Greene Press, 1969.

"Woodstock Railroad Passenger Rates." Leaflet. Woodstock, VT, April 25, 1885.

Wright, Harold. "Genealogy," a document   presented to the author from Mr. Wright's notes. 2006.

CPSIA information can be obtained
at www.ICGtesting.com
Printed in the USA
BVHW080744110620
581224BV00002B/36